LISTENING SPACE

PRAISE FOR LISTENING SPACE

An important contribution to the best literature of problem-solving … great stories and lessons in this entertaining read.

CHARLES C. FOSTER, VICE CHAIR, GEORGE H.W. BUSH FOUNDATION FOR U.S-CHINA RELATIONS; SR. POLICY ADVISOR TO 2000/2004 CAMPAIGNS OF PRESIDENT GEORGE W. BUSH; CHAIRMAN, FOSTERGLOBAL

Barbara Radnofsky reminds us that conflict isn't a bad word. It can be used thoughtfully and compassionately to find common ground, solve stubborn problems and peacefully move societies forward. Within these pages, Barbara powerfully outlines methods and strategies to improve the human experience and build a better world.

HON. JOE KENNEDY III

… demystifies the art and science of productive conversation … a gem.

JIM ESKIN, PRESIDENT, ESKIN FUNDRAISING TRAINING LLC

ALSO BY BARBARA RADNOFSKY

A Citizen's Guide to Impeachment (Melville House, 2017)

Stepping Forward (Lulu, 2007)

The Dancer's Dead (Lulu, 2006)

LISTENING SPACE

A BARBERSHOP GUIDE TO PROBLEM-SOLVING

BARBARA RADNOFSKY

Library of Congress Control Number: 2021921468

ISBN 979-8-498-27245-0

Cover and interior design by Michaela Wood.

All photos at Carlos Barbershop & Beer Garden by Bryan Snook. NASA Apollo 14 public domain photos by Alan Shepard. Photos of Villagomez family from the collection of Carlos Villagomez. Author photo by Dalton DeHart.

To Morris Radnofsky (1896-1960)
U.S. Navy
Commander of American Legion Post in Boston after service in World War I

and

Matthew Radnofsky (1924-1993)
U.S. Army, 306th Bombardment Group
Chief of Crew Systems, NASA Manned Spacecraft Center/Lyndon B. Johnson Space Center

CONTENTS

INTRODUCTION

The best problem-solver I know is a small-town barber named Carlos.

A wise barber-to-the astronauts, starting out in the 1960s and still working today out of his shotgun-shack-of-a-tiny-barbershop, can teach us much about peaceful problem solving, dealing with inevitable conflict in our daily lives. Carlos Villagomez of Webster, Texas entertains with his storytelling as he teaches us to help solve problems. The tales of Carlos the Barber help us analyze why conversations and meals and vacations and dates and meetings and debates and talk shows and campaigns can either degenerate into messy arguments or brawls or turn into positive discussions leading to friendships and peaceful problem-solving. Carlos the Barber, by demonstration and leadership, offers the better way.

During NASA's early days and beyond, barbering from the 1960s through the 2020s in a little town, Carlos counted among his thousands of customers a new generation coming to serve the space program, including six of the seven original astronauts, eight or nine of the Gemini space travelers, and plenty of Apollo faces, including moonwalkers. You could enter the Barbershop, sit in the row of waiting chairs, and listen to out-of-the-world stories. The clientele grew as NASA and the space program grew, including new generations serving the space program and the thriving area growing around it.

Carlos recognizes that efforts to problem-solve may fail because there is no process where the participants can enjoy a space where folks listen and where rules of decency are the norm. The concept is simple: treat everyone fairly and with respect as you listen to them, and they listen to you. This problem-solving process allows everyone involved to shares ideas, consider and test solutions, and ultimately pick what works best for them. The participants – the stakeholders – pick the solutions. Outside a barbershop, the process is called mediation.

The idea of listening and then sharing ideas sounds simple. The great challenge is to create and maintain a place of respect where people will truly listen. Once you provide that listening space, you can identify the problems, and then brainstorm and select solutions.

We can recreate the joy of a barbershop listening space. My job as a professional mediator and a teacher of mediation to children allows me the chance to help create places of respect and listening, with the goal of solving problems. Carlos, the barber whose stories illustrate the principles of mediation in this book, has lived these principles throughout his extraordinary life focused on service to family, friends, country, and strangers. Carlos asked for the forms I use to teach children how to solve problems, so he could aid two friends who asked him for help. He provided them the opportunity to create a special place where they could work on finding solutions. Every day except Sundays, the little Texas business of Carlos Villagomez provides that extraordinary space to his customers.

"Carlos of NASA" is such a local legend that his listening space travels with him; Carlos creates that atmosphere wherever he goes. He is called upon as a storyteller and as a peacemaker for family, friends, strangers dropping in, local businesses in trouble, to advise lawyers, to mentor promising barbers, to deliver medical supplies for children and families, to help elected officials, to serve as friend to law-enforcement, to provide humanitarian relief for the needy.

Carlos has been practicing advanced problem-solving from a very early age in a home with two parents and 15 children, during World War II. He continued serving others and solving problems during his Navy service in Indochina and the life he built in the world of 1960s rural Texas. He peacefully resolved conflicts with the local police department whose renegades threatened Carlos the day before his living space, on the same site as the Barbershop and his newly-opened Beer Garden, was riddled with shotgun blasts. It happened within walking distance of the police station.

This book introduces you to the community of bikers and cowboys and farmers and NASA employees and Chamber of Commerce/Rotary buddies and local lawyers and business leaders who have peacefully coexisted and benefitted from a kind barber's help. Carlos' problem-solving and intelligent advocacy peacefully resolved problems benefitting his own businesses and those of his friendly competitors beyond the town of Webster. He's helped businesses from nearby Maribelle's Bar on the Kemah waterfront to every bar nationwide stocked with Coors Beer, as he persuaded Adolph Coors to change his business practices on more than one occasion, to better results for everyone involved.

We can learn, as well, the dangers to peaceful problem solving when we mistakenly allow arguments to go far beyond respectful listening. Carlos tells the story on himself, describing when our favorite barber intervened too late. Just as barbers found themselves called to medical service in centuries past, Carlos found himself patching up a post-fight customer with solid doctoring skills.

The stories of Carlos the Barber illustrate a well-lived life of service. These barbershop chats also explain why the compact, tidy shack is so handsomely decorated with souvenirs from his customers when they return from space travel, from the 1960s to the present.

Carlos, now in his vibrant eighties, is constantly learning, seeking education and information. He retains a keen curiosity. Other than active-duty service on a Navy warship on jungle rivers and open sea in Indochina in the aftermath of World War II, Carlos has been a barber and businessman his entire adult life. He's proud of his many grandchildren, all at various stages, including a granddaughter who is a Master Chief in the Navy. Carlos' many brilliant sisters had to quit their formal education at eighth grade. To a woman, each persisted and ultimately found ways to gain education as adults. Their successes are due to transitioning through life, adapting, and progressing via skills learned, hard work, discipline, and self-betterment.

You will nowadays find Jesse Salinas, taken under Carlos' wing and a Master Barber in his own right, working alongside Carlos, carrying on the traditions. Jesse provides many of the tales of the younger astronauts in his chair and arranged for interviews for more details. Jesse spends his spare time in humanitarian good works in the Galveston Bay Area and planning a run for City Council, under the guidance of former Webster City Councilman and Mayor Pro Tem Carlos.

From the 1960s to present day 2020s, Carlos has been helping his friends in a very special place near the intersection of what used-to-be NASA Road One and Old Galveston Road. And he helps far beyond. You will learn of his lifelong, closest friendship with the first American in space, traveling with him in more earthly pursuits, and discover the gifts famed spaceman Admiral Alan Shepard brought to Carlos from his outer space and moon explorations. Enjoy the stories of Neil Armstrong, the first human to set foot on the moon, as he benefitted from Carlos' resourcefulness, advice, and experience. Admire Jesse's customer, Space Shuttle Commander and Vietnam War hero Michael Coats teaching everyone in the Barbershop the long-term impacts to the astronaut corps and NASA from a special mediation which put this esteemed astronaut back into space.

This book is a guide to peaceful problem solving. The key is listening with respect – or at least working to create that appearance with important gestures of respect. When we create that appearance of listening, we find ourselves and others truly listening.

Children and adults can create a neutral, protected environment with agreed ground rules for respectful conduct in everyday life. You need not be a born peacemaker or listener. Few people are! But everyone, with a bit of practice, can learn to listen actively, make peace, and model skills such as "Active Listening" or "Try to Put Yourself in Their Shoes." We can model Carlos' skills of listening carefully, with quiet and close attention. By his example, he teaches both creative thinking and critical thinking. He creates a listening space where warring parties can consider and decide their own fate without some authoritarian declaring a winner.

Congratulate yourself if you can come to agreement on a mediation process with ground rules, even without solving every problem. Creating a peaceful place is a worthy achievement, akin to the worthy goals of building good relationships and atmospheres in modern societies. Both children and adults function best, according to studies referenced in this book, when they play and work under conditions which support their sense of control, autonomy, importance, and worth. That is the atmosphere of mediation!

The book provides *Appendices* and *Answers to Frequently Asked Questions*. There is no penalty for jumping to the back of the book for these answers, exercises, and checklists, but you will miss plenty of stories and lessons learned from Carlos, Jesse, and the customers they are proud to serve.

Carlos uses his strengths – his intelligence, his warm smile, sense of humor and storytelling abilities – to promote trust and listening. When Carlos listens, others talk. He gives them that opportunity to speak, never interrupting, and then helps them peacefully analyze problems and brainstorm solutions.

In his gentle ways, Carlos uses his considerable "critical" thinking skills. Many people assume the word "critical" means we must be negative, angry, thoughtlessly lashing out or attacking ideas we don't like or understand. To the contrary, "critical" thinking requires a calm, thoughtful hearing, questioning, and analysis of information from many sources. We can all learn how to better create and conduct a process where we discover and exchange valuable information and insight, learn and listen, then thoughtfully list and test solutions to see how proposed solutions might work in practice.

In using this book, please know it contains no legal advice. Consult and involve a lawyer for legal implications and laws, including confidentiality and use of mediators in dispute resolution, as well as the process and effects on your organization. Most importantly, do not try to mediate if there is any sense of danger.

Why do students of all ages enjoy learning the skills of mediation? Mediation techniques can help the participants develop life skills serving their needs. A mediation does not always bring about a concrete solution – but participants experience the great reward and comfort of building a space providing respect and dignity. That is the feeling in the barber chair of Carlos Villagomez or Jesse Salinas. We can each help create a special atmosphere of respect, a listening space, leading to peaceful solutions.

1

THE STORY OF CARLOS

Carlos' most famous hair appointment was no surprise; it was scheduled well in advance. Carlos had already visited his friend Alan Shepard's home to cut the astronaut's hair before the Apollo 14 moon mission and knew he would be seeing Shepard immediately after the mission. Shepard was Carlos' closest friend in the astronaut corps.

America's first man in space in 1961 had experienced a dashing career as one of the first pilots flying from and landing onto naval carriers, as a talented test pilot, and as one of the nation's original Mercury astronauts. Shepard had then been sidelined from flight after developing Meniere's disease, which affects hearing and balance.

Still, the famed spaceman persevered; he stayed at NASA with administrative functions, including Chief of the Astronaut Office, hoping he could beat the disease and be allowed to fly. He did. The future Admiral Shepard would become the only one of the famous Original Mercury Seven to eventually walk on the moon. In 1968, Shepard learned of experimental surgery. Driven by hope of a cure to get back into space, he underwent the risky operation in Los Angeles. In six months, the symptoms disappeared. His restoration to flight status in May 1969 (plus rumored assignment-jockeying) led to his moon-walking assignment to Apollo 14 in January-February 1971.

After extensive mission training, the astronauts were required to enter a pre-mission, three-week quarantine. The night before quarantine, Carlos brought his trusty barber shears to Shepard's home. The happy astronaut guided Carlos through the night sky, as they shared drinks, talked life, and made plans for the next haircut. Shepard, a life-long friend to Carlos, was particular about his look. The 47-year-old Mission Commander of Apollo 14 was in great shape, boyishly handsome, a sharp dresser, and wore his hair in a popular full businessman's haircut, carefully developed, designed, trimmed and maintained by the astronaut and his barber friend.

That evening, at the astronaut's home before the start of the mission, Carlos cut his friend's hair far shorter than usual in anticipation of the long pre-mission quarantine, moon travel, work on the surface, return to Earth, and isolation afterward. The barber promised his availability as soon as Shepard was released from isolation.

What Carlos did not know was that Commander Shepard would call him on the way back to Earth, personally confirming the first-ever hair appointment from space, as NASA patched through the headline-making phone call. Shepard put Carlos on the map. The barber received massive international media attention and immediately recognized the potential. He planned and executed an expansion. The Barbershop shifted venues for a time and grew to multiple chairs as he increased his clientele well beyond NASA and Webster locals. When the excitement faded, he still had the news articles decoupaged onto wood plaques by his loved ones, in the style of the 1960s. Carlos was able to efficiently shrink the business, too. Now well into his eighties, Carlos still prepares for every important task; his strengths include an embrace of flexibility and the ability to turn surprises to advantages.

After his Apollo 14 mission, Alan Shepard did indeed follow the plan outlined with Carlos and drove straight to the Barbershop upon release from the isolation facility. The moonwalker was still in his post-mission NASA flight-suit. One of the most famous faces in the world wanted complete privacy until Carlos cut and styled his fast-growing hair. The careful astronaut insisted that Carlos lock the door so no one would see him parked under the bubble of the hair dryer needed to ensure that his longish hairstyle was perfectly coiffed and "permed," and would remain chemically so, until the next hair appointment.

How did Carlos arrive at the doorstep of NASA, receiving the history-making haircut appointment call from outer space covered by the world press?

Carlos Villagomez was part of a huge family born to hard-working parents who also raised others' children in the family home. They believed that "everyone needs a trade." His parents offered two possible occupations for Carlos: barber or cobbler. While Carlos is also a skilled shoemaker, everyone, including Carlos, favored barbering for the talented boy.

Carlos' family made their home, filled with two parents and 15 active children, near the Ship Channel in the "wards" of Houston, during the early part of the twentieth century. Their Magnolia Park neighborhood was the place for World War I émigrés from Mexico and their children. Magnolia Park today remains a tight-knit community centered on family and heritage. Papá Villagomez worked hard at a large cement company for 44 years. Carlos was born between the World Wars, on May 20,1936. He recalls that his mother "spent her life in the kitchen and was always feeding a baby."

Carlos' family lost one baby, Margarita, to tuberculosis. They raised more than their own 13 remaining children. In hard times, especially in the time of rampant TB, the family took in two more children permanently. These youngsters, too, took the Villagomez name. Carlos stays in touch with them and their families. After all, he is their big brother.

The Villagomez home, with one bathroom and an entire neighborhood of family inside, had its fair share of conflict within. The boys used an outdoor shower and privy, with the addition of running hot and cold water, thanks to Papá's obtaining large hot-water heaters from old Ellington Air Force Base. When the children learned English, "Papá" became "Dad." Their mother never learned English, so she remained "Mamá." Carlos remembers Mamá telling him, "Your Papá is working himself to death so we can be fed."

Papá built an apartment over the garage. The small, safe, private area housed folks who had nowhere else to go. Over the years, the Villagomez home and apartment served as refuge for many people in conflict, several of Carlos' grown sisters with their babies, and the children of others in need. Carlos lived there a bit after he returned from distinguished Navy service on the other side of the world.

All the Villagomez boys enlisted in the services as soon as they got out of school. Carlos chose the Navy for himself. He's justifiably proud of his service. He speaks of his love for the Navy and how he especially enjoyed working with ships and handling boats, including his Captain's gig, having earned the Captain's great trust. (If you go for a haircut, stay for the story of how AWOL sailors stole the Captain's gig). Young Carlos called home to tell Mamá she should have all of the boys choose the Navy for enlistment. "Tell them," he insisted, "tell them all. I love the Navy. I love the food, there's always enough to eat, tell the boys to choose Navy. The food is great!"

From 1953 to 1957, Carlos served on a dock landing warship, the USS Comstock LSD-19, in Indochina during the Korean conflict, amidst much fighting in the aftermath of WWII. During that time, his wife delivered their first-born child, a boy. He never saw his wife during her pregnancy or when his son was born. He remembers with loving pride meeting Carlos, Jr. as a two-month-old baby.

In what is now Vietnam, the warship's missions included moving the fleeing Catholic population from the north to the south. The ship and its crew saved thousands of people, including a physicist who walked into the Barbershop years later. The scientist realized that Carlos had been a sailor on the ship that saved what remained of his family. The man asked Carlos to stay late, please, at the shop. To Carlos' surprise, the customer returned later that evening with his sister and aged, blind mother who brought a most treasured photo with them. It was a picture of the ship that had saved their lives.

The father of the family had disappeared and never made it aboard the warship; this now-grown man and his family wanted Carlos to know the difference the U.S. Navy and his service made in their lives. The little boy saved by the U.S. Navy had become a scientist, his older brother a respected veterinarian, and his big sister a fine teacher. Carlos reminisced later that the warship would open its huge ramp as enemy bullets flew, pelting the ship and each crowd of escapees, who came running as fast as they could into the safety of the warship, secure only when the ramp lifted behind them, blocking the barrage of bullets.

In Korea, the ship's important missions included evacuation of U.S. soldiers to the Japanese coast. Carlos developed painful ringing in the ears from the surrounding, noisy enemy fire as the soldiers would run aboard. He explained he just learned to live with it, as he does to this day.

The warship carried equipment, Marines, and Navy frogmen. The ship would approach land in routinely rough seas to launch frogmen on their missions. Carlos marveled at the Navy frogmen's abilities to jump from the ship traveling at speeds of 15 to 20 knots. These predecessors to the modern SEALS encountered 20-foot waves, made the arduous swim to shore, conducted their missions, and calmly returned at the appointed hour. Those were the men Carlos admired although he never knew the details of the missions of the frogmen. These men told Carlos that it was all in a day's work and something "you just get used to."

Carlos volunteered as a test subject to determine the effects of dropping an atomic bomb during tests at the Enewetak Atoll in the Marshall Islands. Carlos recalled being told that the Navy wanted to test what would happen to a ship and its occupants within 2 to 3 miles of an atomic explosion. Carlos says the effects were "spectacular." That old test ship shook, pipes broke, the blast waves and wake were huge, and the scope and effect of the water spout and stem of the mushroom cloud even more extraordinary. Eventually, Carlos' test ship sank. He received a certificate for his service as a volunteer subject. Years later, the Navy followed up with him, asked about his experiences during this period in Indochina, and offered him partial disability, they said, for his lifelong ear problems.

Early in his life, an event shaped Carlos' outlook on decision-making. One of Carlos' older sisters received the sad news that the boy she loved deeply, whom she was engaged to marry, was lost in World War II. She eventually married another man. When her long-lost fiancé returned years later from prisoner-of-war camp, the family priest dictated what would happen to Carlos' sister. She must remain with her current husband and abandon her long-lost fiancé. She sadly complied with the solution imposed upon her. Carlos has never forgotten the impact of that conflict resolution on his beloved sister's life. She had no control, no voice to be heard, no autonomy. No one was willing to listen to her. The life-changing decision was dictated to the young woman. Carlos always remembers how her loss of control over this life-changing decision left his sister powerless and devastated. She was offered no choice.

Carlos learned much about life and managing conflict through challenging life experiences, particularly the triumphs and sufferings of people he admired and loved. He has personal experience that if you can successfully create and maintain an atmosphere of respect with a fair process (the decision-making process the parties feel is "due" to them, also known as "due process"), a human being will be more likely to accept a less-than-perfect solution, so long as their voices were fairly considered or they volunteered to participate.

We owe it to folks in happy times and, especially in times of stress, to be treated with respect. When you allow a person to fairly participate in the decisions that will affect their lives, whether decisions involve annulling a marriage or resolving a business dispute where hard-earned money is at stake, they will more likely abide by the decision and work towards enforcing it. Carlos understands the value of treating people with respect.

After returning from the service, Carlos found a job with Norris of Houston, a famous hairdresser. Carlos served the Houston business as a manager in the 1960s. But he didn't enjoy the work and was looking to move on. He spoke with a friend, Gene Horton, the press relations officer from NASA.

In the 1960s, NASA had deliberately set out to form and grow a vibrant society surrounding the Space Center built on a cow pasture. Carlos' press friend at NASA asked, "Why don't you move to the NASA area? We're growing and we need someone, not just to cut hair, but also talk to our folks and become a part of the community."

Carlos drove south to the now-modernizing but still largely rural area near the modern buildings composing the Manned Spacecraft Center. This was a site which had been chosen with thanks in large part due to the power and influence of then-Vice President Lyndon B. Johnson, who as a powerful Senator had sponsored the law creating NASA. The Center was renamed in the next decade in honor of the late President Johnson, in 1973.

Carlos found the town hotel. It was a Holiday Inn, where what Carlos describes as a "hippie hairdresser" had been renting a hotel room for various endeavors, including barbering, but had then left town. When Carlos saw the room, he was startled to find the remnants of some type of strange, abandoned clinic, a dental chair and various dental devices which had all somehow been converted to use as a barbershop, complete with that strange chair. Carlos explains that he had never seen anything like it and said to himself "Whoa…" Moreover, the hotel demanded a $200 deposit, presumably for possible damage to the remnants of the dental clinic. Carlos always looks on the bright side of life. On further, optimistic thought, he eventually bargained for a month-to-month lease of $240/month with the Holiday Inn's condition that he would have to leave if the hotel ever needed that room. He paid the deposit, left his safe managerial job, and came to NASA to work with the pioneers who were still answering the late President John Kennedy's call to put a man on the moon before the end of the decade.

Word of Carlos' skills and abilities spread quickly among the NASA community. He worked and saved. Two years later, he needed both more air conditioning and more space, and the Holiday Inn had neither. He had to move on. He turned this forced move to advantage, finding a rambling, old boarding house in the town of Webster, best known then as a speed trap where most experienced truckers knew to slow down as they plowed through. When Carlos moved in, boarders still occupied many of the 14 rooms.

Within a few years, the boarders had drifted on, replaced in each room by barbers who knew or heard of the entrepreneurial barber. Carlos welcomed the diverse barbers to set up their unique shops in the various boarder rooms, each decorated in distinctive style. During the late sixties and early seventies, Carlos and his barbers became members of the community of farmers, industry workers, ranch hands, bikers, country folk, service people, engineers, and aerospace contractors now outnumbering NASA government employees, who had originally settled locally in new subdivisions nestled near lakes and old bait shops, roadhouses, cow pastures, and newly arrived businesses.

Carlos bought a switchboard, which helped in making appointments and profits by selling answering services and private line connections to over 100 customers. He staffed that old-fashioned switchboard with an operator twenty-four hours a day, seven days a week.

Other entrepreneurs flocked in, too, hoping to capitalize on the emergence of a space city. The main drag was NASA Road One, a street which would be flooded by subsidence and the lake it crosses, rebuilt every so often and ultimately replaced by what you can visit now via a fancy, broad ribbon of concrete. A few years later, Carlos further developed the large piece of property surrounding the aging boarding house, which he eventually demolished. You will find the property around Webster, Texas, on Old Galveston Road. That old road has been enlarged over the decades and is now more commonly known as Highway Three.

To this day, Carlos cuts hair from a tiny "shotgun" shack on the property. Yes, you can literally shoot through the front door and the shotgun pellets will go through the back door.

The town of Webster needed to outgrow its traffic trap status. People in the town saw that need, recognized Carlos' potential, and asked him to help. He spoke to the then-police chief and Mayor, but his first efforts met with failure. People with power and town old-timers held to the cowboy, wild west mentality; law enforcement and fire department were dominated by men who felt they were the law. Such men felt no need for input from the populace. They had no respect for elected officials or their appointed chiefs who failed to defer to the old guard.

It was around the same time that Carlos decided to use a good part of his property to develop the Beer Garden, which enjoyed immediate popularity. Carlos' Beer Garden was (and remains) a stone's throw from the Webster Police Department. Rogue Webster police officers were not pleased with an entrepreneurial Mr. Carlos Villagomez, and they worked to make business and life difficult for their neighbor.

One evening, heavily armed local police burst into the new Beer Garden, waving pistols, and wielding their shotguns as one officer drew his finger across his neck in a slicing gesture. "Cut the noise!" they screamed. They menaced the customers, too, threatening them with jail. It was a fearsome scene for the NASA engineers, businessman, hardworking Texas City plant workers, ranch hands, and bikers gathered at the Beer Garden.

Carlos remembers the wild scene.

"What did I do? They were threatening my customers and my bar people! So, I snuck out the back and ran to the Mayor's house. I knew the Mayor would be fair, even though he wasn't that happy when I tried to get a license to sell beer in my place next to a police station. The City Council had been divided, three yeses and three nos. The Mayor hadn't liked the idea. But I remembered: the Mayor had said that, if I operated within the law, a man should be entitled to sell beer there. He had voted yes and that's how I got my license. He was my best chance." Carlos reflected on this time with a chuckle as he described his decision-making, wondering how the mayor would react.

"When I ran over to the Mayor's house that night and told him what happened, he was angry! Yes, he was really angry, but it was anger at those threatening, renegade cops. The next morning, he called them in to his office and fired those renegades. And the Mayor wrote a letter to the Chamber of Commerce folks telling them they should welcome me."

The Mayor's willingness to accept the determined Carlos and his new Beer Garden was not matched by the entire community.

"Back then, I was living on top of the old boarding house. That same night, someone shot up the place, the doors. Man, they shotgunned all over the whole front. My switchboard operator was working the night shift, on the first floor. They could have killed him! These people were really hurting business."

The police chief came to talk to Carlos the next day, as Carlos was assessing the damage, Carlos recalls. "He begged me, 'Please don't call the FBI.' I knew they'd fired those cops, so I paid for the damage they caused. No one else would do it. And I repaired the mess they made."

Carlos had made his decision. He would keep the roots he had planted in the NASA community, reaching back to the 1960s. "I told them I wasn't going away. That was in the early 1980s; that's when I decided I needed to help this town change. So I ran for City Council. The first time I lost by one vote. But then, a councilman resigned, and the Mayor appointed me because, well, I lost by one vote. I was the logical choice. So, I was then put on the Council. After that I got reelected and then they made me Mayor pro tem."

Carlos learned much serving on City Council and serving as Mayor pro tem. He also joined the Rotary Club and well-meaning groups and sought out wise people to learn how good government can best function, particularly on a city or town level.

He recollects using what he learned. "We needed a strong manager form of government, a person with a spirit, experience and expertise who wouldn't leave after an election cycle. So, I strongly suggested to the council and mayor that we adopt a strong manager form. I proposed we amend our documents, and it was first disputed. And we debated it some more.

"But then, it passed!"

Carlos recounts the arduous search, bitterly resisted by the old timers, for a truly independent manager. He found a great one, out of state. Carlos spent much time providing information to the expert Manager, who listened and carefully examined the town's books and records. The Manager understood from his review how the town of Webster had been operating, renegades and crooks included. The City Manager also taught Carlos about methods and process for economic development.

Carlos speaks efficiently and eloquently about the importance and detailed functions of accounting in various City departments. The City Manager, he explains, "started to investigate those officials in our fire department who were supposed to be keeping proper records. He learned that two of the trucks had been confiscated by the IRS, and the fire department wasn't even in possession of equipment it claimed." The City Manager also helped Carlos learn about methods and practices of economic development.

What happened next? Carlos recalls, "I revealed a massive scandal in the Fire Department to the City Council and, since I was also Mayor pro tem, we were able to pass a tax for infrastructure and business development which still aids our current city team. It is great for development. We created the Webster Economic Development Board. I'm very happy about what happened to the city of Webster."

Carlos, now in his 80s, remains on the Webster Economic Development Board and treasures the businesses and roads, solidly built homes, sidewalks, and exciting new developments, all resisted by the old-timers. Carlos' leadership in the community is one reason why, on any given day, you might exit the Barbershop and step into the Beer Garden and have a burger and fries with the President of the Bay Area/Houston Economic Partnership, visiting with Carlos and local church leaders about the Spaceport and a long list of developments in the now thriving region.

After the early days of space exploration, Carlos cut the hair of many female astronauts and friends within the new groups within the astronaut corps; he was glad to see the growing diversity. He grieved mightily after the Challenger Disaster when he learned what had happened to his friends. He recalled with much fondness that, not long before the disaster, an exuberant female astronaut on that flight had visited with buddies and borrowed billiard balls from the Beer Garden pool table for a scientific experiment in space.

In his heyday, Carlos cut the hair of press, dignitaries, and many women enjoying boyish styles. He cut actress Mia Farrow's hair when she and Andre Previn lived in Houston. In his eighties, he still cuts the hair, or watches with care as Jesse cuts the hair and eyebrows of everyday heroes from local homes, hospitals, schools, hotels, farms, businesses, and bustling life around the Johnson Space Center south of Houston.

Carlos earned his place as an integral pillar of the community.

Not long ago, Carlos was asked to step into a long-standing disagreement. He did not want to abandon his two friends who were embroiled in a bitter business dispute involving strongly held personal feelings of right and wrong, fairness, and a lot of hard-earned money.

He asked for a quick crash-course in mediation.

2

CARLOS, WE HAVE A PROBLEM

Local businessmen agreed they should ask Carlos to help solve their problem. They trust him. For many people, unaware of Carlos' early life, their trust is not based on his past, growing up by the Ship Channel or serving his country on the other side of the world in Indochina. They know he lives in the NASA area, is friend and confidante to the wide-ranging community, and has served in elective office as a respected public servant. They may recognize him for his wife's tamales; for over four decades his family and staff have given away her traditional Christmas tamales to countless thousands of hungry people.

Carlos and the businessmen prepared well and agreed to a problem-solving meeting. The mediation process described in this book worked. Carlos asked for my booklet developed over the last forty-plus years, including my simple forms, ordinarily used in teaching mediation classes in public and private schools, reproduced in the Appendices. The guide covers the basics for children, of all ages, including children with special needs, who become particularly strong mediators, working with much empathy. The booklet also provides explanations for parents and teachers on what to expect, and how to help, as children work in teams to resolve problems with fellow students, setting ground rules and creating a protected space for listening, talking, brainstorming solutions, and selecting the solutions which work best for them.

Carlos read the pamphlet and forms, asked a few questions, then set out on his mission. He made sure that the businessmen who were participating had the power to make an agreement and that they agreed to the basics, including the basic Ground Rules for respectful conduct, keeping things confidential, and carrying out their agreement. The booklet intended for children worked for grown-ups, too.

Life experience taught Carlos much of what he needed to know. His life story illustrates the many, different qualities we seek in honorable, effective leadership. When Carlos come to Webster, he dealt with much conflict. His responses shaped his reputation. His NASA area life and contributions are well-known and count for much. Local businessmen seeking Carlos as peacemaker knew much of this Webster history of Carlos. He agreed to help. Drawing on his life experiences, Carlos quickly learned mediation basics.

Carlos prepared well for his mediation. When I asked later why he asked for my simple teaching handbook and forms given his high community standing, life experiences and expertise, Carlos gave a revealing answer, replying simply, "I wanted to learn. To get it better. Your handbook helped a lot."

His many outstanding traits include humility, courage, curiosity, thirst for knowledge – and a caring for his fellow man such that he earns the significant trust the community places in him. His community knows Carlos will indeed try his best when helping folks in need. He understood the mediation concepts which allow a good leader to help the participants to find solutions to problems. Mediation seeks no findings of guilt, innocence, or some universal "truth."

Carlos recognized we can solve problems and resolve conflicts, despite remaining disagreements, which may never be resolved. The process of mediation moves to the distinct stage of "Solutions" only after the participants identify, discuss, and accept disagreements, acknowledged as part of life. But first, the parties must get ready for the process.

Learn the Basics

The basics are outlined in the "Mediator's Cheat Sheet" in Appendix D. Mediation involves two steps, after an important introduction and agreement to ground rules.

Here are the steps:

- **Step One: Identify the Problem**
- **Step Two: Solve the Problem**

The parties use Step One to communicate with each other, actively listening with good body language, showing respect, and using thoughtful questions. The parties usually take a break and then move forward to Step Two to brainstorm solutions with creative ideas, without attacking the suggestions. Instead, the participants write them down to analyze later. When the mediation participants finish brainstorming ideas, they look at the list and use critical thinking to choose the best solution. With critical thinking, they ask questions such as "how will it solve the problem and work in real practice" and "what are the disadvantages this suggestion could cause."

Plan

Use whatever time you have to think and plan. As you plan, you will acquire insight into all participants' thought processes, relationships, levels of trust, and many external factors which can affect the outcome of discussions, negotiations, or formal mediation. Once you have a handle on how your side and the other side think, you will be able also to develop a realistic idea of "what is success" for you and for others. Try to come to agreement with your group on what are the mileposts towards success for you and for the other parties. Preparation and consideration of these issues from each side's standpoint allows you to adjust your strategy and tactics to new information.

While planning, gather your team with a purpose:

identify and list your problems and goals, and then do the same for the other party. Gather and consider information about yourself and the other parties for any discussion, negotiation, or mediation. Be open to all legitimate mechanisms of information gathering. Listening is a key ingredient. As you gather information and analyze it, you will want to take notes and make lists.

You should be open to information gathering and reliability-testing throughout the entirety of the preparation and mediation process. Here are Questions to help preparation:

- Who are the participants and how do they process information and decide? Seek answers to such questions as: Are they impulsive, emotional, risk takers, analytical, conservative? Are they stakeholders in the dispute, with their conduct in question, causing them to defend the positions previously taken, with no flexibility? Are they resolute for other reasons?
- What is the level of resolve, and what factors affect the resolve not to compromise?
- What are the relationships involved? Is this a personal or business relationship? Is it ongoing or one time? What have been and what are the contemplated levels of interaction?
- Can you trust the sources and information received? What is the level of reliability?

Remember, the other group will also evaluate your

side and your positions. They also seek answers to these questions. Many parties or disputants are interested in levels of resolve on each side. If you are a disputant, consider your own attitude as well as the other side. How resolute are you? What appearance of resolve have you created? Do the individuals acting for their organization have the same goals as the organization?[1]

One goal everyone can list is to prevent sliding from the Solutions stage back into re-hashing issues. Help the leaders in their difficult roles to move forward through the step. Help the leadership make progress and stick to the plan. Help your leaders, too, in recognizing when a solution has been found! Many times, the solution is simpler than folks want to admit.

The key to using any of the information you carefully gather is putting yourself in the shoes of the other party. Empathy – the ability to understand what another being is experiencing or feeling without being told – is an important life skill. Empathy is a key to successful negotiation and mediation.

You may think the key issue is: "What do we want and need?" The key to getting what you need, however, is finding out: "What does the other side want and need?" The best way to find the answer to this key question is to practice by putting yourself in the other sides' place and make their arguments for them.

Practice

Within an hour of practice, with simple exercises, you will feel at ease in creating an inspiring and wonderful atmosphere of dignity and respect, with everyone agreed to enforce the ground rules. This mediation process is now a common, solution-oriented process, used throughout the world. The process involves no judging of who is right or wrong. No judge or jury will decide the solution in a mediation.

Put yourself and your colleagues in the frame of mind to learn the use of a powerful tool, which you will configure to meet your needs. It is a process applicable in all situations involving international conflicts; military planning; lawsuits in any stage; school playgrounds, classrooms and lunchroom disputes; quiet business conference rooms; and non-profits seeking ways to find common ground.

Within a short time, children can explain the two-step process of mediation. They use the same process used by Carlos and professional mediators.

I teach mediation to children with everyone's understanding that the children will demonstrate their skills to their peers, families, and school faculty and administration at the end of the course. The great motivation for many of the students is performing well in a school-wide demonstration, a well-rehearsed duplication of an in-class play-acting exercise. Students who have never said a word in front of a large audience will stand and square their shoulders, if they can. They will then appear to carefully listen to a question (which they've written in class), and then reply with an answer (which they've carefully considered and rehearsed for weeks). Many time the answer is simply a firm "yes" or a particular concept, such as the words "eye contact!" conveyed in whatever manner the child can best communicate.

Each student leaves the demonstration with a memory of a successful, well-received presentation of one idea the student will never forget. Every child is entitled to the proud memory and confidence of having presented valuable knowledge to their friends, teachers, and parents who have all taken the time to watch the presentations.

In schools, student mediators practice "mock" mediations and use other creative exercises in class to build friendships among the participants as they practice. The activities place participants into the shoes and posture of someone else, building empathy and giving each side great understanding about the other party. We can practice thinking about how the other side thinks in addition to researching facts about the other side.

To best convey your needs effectively, and to convince the other side of your resolve, you will benefit in knowing how they will react to your presentation. So, practice by listening carefully to someone presenting your position. In mock exercises, you can also practice working with a note-taker, a "scribe,' to learn how you can best understand and remember and repeat someone else's ideas fairly and concisely, without judging. The Appendices suggest exercises using body language to prove you are listening, not interrupting, and using questions to reword what you've heard in order to prove you are trying to understand, not to argue.

As you learn more about yourself and your organization by trying to place yourself in the other side's frame of mind, you may see that you cannot always trust the information you think you obtained on any particular issue. In role playing, you can determine whether you have any idea of the other side's underlying desires or their levels of resolve.

General Eisenhower famously taught that plans are useless, but planning is indispensable. We can learn about alternatives and gain the flexibility to adapt our plan using scenarios simulating real life experience. Planning and practice for conflict resolution yields helpful information in peacetime as well as in warfare.

Carlos studied the children's forms and mediated his friends' dispute to the great satisfaction and now-blooming friendship of each person involved. He has been asked to step in as a neutral, fair mediator in other disputes as well. Carlos witnessed a major change following the resolution of the disputes. There was a kindness, rather than bitterness, by the participants towards each other and their families. This led to even greater good works in the community. Warring businessmen found a listening space where fairness and gestures of respect in the process extended benefit to other businesses.

Where once misunderstandings and anger caused enduring arguments, now, good feelings and mutual assistance between rivals prevail. As inevitably happens in life, a related conflict developed, and the businessmen plus a new disputant approached Carlos to help again. The group skillfully, peacefully, and quickly resolved the related conflict.

The businessman who paid the most took everyone involved to lunch to celebrate the resolution.

3

RESPECT THE PROCESS

Good leaders protect and foster respect for the process of problem solving. If everyone agrees that the decision-making process is fair, they will more likely accept the solution. Of course, people involved in disputes do not always turn to formalized processes. The concept still works! For example, if everyone agrees that an influential, respected figure is trusted to resolve a disagreement and all parties agree to such a community leader's role as decision-maker, the result is very likely to be accepted and honored.

Carlos' dad Augustin Villagomez was a respected, wise man in his world. Papá clearly understood and accepted the power of an acknowledged leader in his family and the close-knit community in which he lived. He solved problems with an elegant sense of justice and a deep understanding of human nature.

Carlos' father developed the ability to understand what others were thinking and feeling, just as his son developed those skills. The elder Villagomez was of a different time and place. Augustin Villagomez possessed an old-world sense of honor. His long-time employer, Lone Star Cement, recognized the respected worker's lifelong, enduring dedication with a gold watch.

Mr. and Mrs. Villagomez greatly valued the honor and sacrifices the gold watch represented. Mr. Villagomez took it off only to shower at the plant, an important privilege the cement company permitted such a valued, long-time employee. One day while in the shower at work, someone stole the watch, laid with his other belongings.

What dismay when Mr. Villagomez told his wife of the theft! Mrs. Villagomez, who had such pride and felt she best knew what sacrifices and service the stolen watch represented, was particularly and deeply, visibly affected. Her husband suffered silently.

Many years later, after a Mass and priestly admonition to treat a fellow man fairly, a former co-worker and fellow congregant came to the house to both confess the watch theft to the elder Mr. Villagomez and to return the stolen, prized possession. The thief was well-convinced he must make proper amends or suffer the severest of penalties in the afterlife. The thief returned the watch.

Mr. Villagomez held the watch. He handed it back to the thief. "You will wear it," he said, "and tell your wife and co-workers what you did."

A Fair Process Deserves Protection

If you are in a group or organization with a problem, you may have a choice of who to call for help in a mediation. The process begins with your own people, who will learn, model, and teach how to convey respect. In deciding on participants, take special care with decision-makers who were directly involved in the dispute. These people may feel the need to defend their conduct at all costs. Those folks are not traditionally good listeners. It is hard for anyone to be impartial, objective, or reasonable when their conduct is questioned or if they feel criticized. Look for decision-makers willing to participate who may be known for their listening skills, critical thinking, and reason.

With mediation, we seek leaders able to create and maintain an environment where each participant understands the importance of observing, listening, gathering and evaluating information, then clearly moving on to brainstorming, followed by testing solutions to now meet better-understood needs.

A Short Course on Due Process

The bottom line, particularly and proudly in the United States of America, is that the process you design, choose, and follow will matter very much. Here is a quick lesson in the American ideal of *due process*.

The Constitution – the supreme law of our United States – provides that no person shall "be deprived of life, liberty, or property, without due process of law." This concept of "due process" is provided to us twice in the Constitution.

Due process – the process which is due to us – means much in terms of fairness. Notably (for preservation of our democratic institutions, in our way of life, and in mediation), we are entitled to fairness in notice of important matters facing us and a meaningful opportunity to be heard. So due process is shorthand for the fair process we are each due as a matter of justice.

The process can include, but does not require, a professional, neutral mediator. It should always include respected and thoughtful participants from each side, each willing to work together to create an atmosphere of respect.

Find the genuine people in your community who can train themselves to use the process. Mediation participants learn how to think better — creatively, and then critically — and to model and teach these skills in a special, protected environment.

Recognize Good Leadership Qualities

If you are working on behalf of a group, consider suggesting that each organization involved in the problems discussion select a leader from inside each group. Leaders will help create the atmosphere of listening. The parties together can alternatively or additionally agree on an outsider to assist, looking for someone regarded as neutral. Such neutral leadership requires perseverance in creating and maintaining a calm, non-violent enforcement of ground rules and the protected space.

Look for persons willing to learn and improve themselves in demonstrating neutrality, tenacity, ability to scribe, empathy, flexibility, open-mindedness, cordiality, eternal vigilance, good communication skills, and good judgment. We all realize no one is perfect, and you can help your leaders who have human weaknesses, reminding and encouraging them to stay with the program throughout the process. Regardless of whether your leaders are designated to act as mediator, or will be instead supporting the process, choose folks with a variety of abilities. No one embodies all, of course.

- *Neutrality* - If you chose a leader to serve both sides as Mediator, they need to stay neutral. Impartiality is difficult, even in play-acting. It is hard not to judge or take sides! A good "neutral" must learn and model listening skills and demonstrate maturity in actively leading the process through stages without backsliding into an earlier stage of the discussion. A neutral leader will encourage active listening through body language or repetition to show that a listener can hear and listen; understand; and respect the speaker and process, by remaining quiet or making limited use of questions, to reinforce that they are indeed listening. While encouraging each side to tell their story, the leaders watch the timing and rhythm of the process. They plan for transitioning to a separate stage where the parties will "brainstorm," proposing a variety of solutions which are captured in list form. After concluding the storm-of-ideas meeting, the leaders act as neutrals and not as partisans, guiding the disputants to test their proposals ("How would that work?"). Then, leaders help the parties to choose the best solution to meet the needs of the participants. The parties may need reminders that they agreed to ground rules to maintain an atmosphere of respect and to document the agreed solution to the problem.

- *Tenacity* - A great leader works through difficult times and knows when to ignore the posturing of the nay-sayers, while not insulting the speaker. Your leaders must be prepared to help maintain a protected space of respect and dedication, demonstrating calm perseverance in securing agreement to the Ground Rules in the beginning and then properly enforcing the Ground Rules. The leaders may well have to repeatedly remind the participants they have agreed to the Ground Rules at various heated moments during the mediation.

- *Ability to Scribe* - If each party has a representative co-leading the discussion, you have found a person who will respect and work with a co-leader and who will follow and fairly enforce the ground rules. Perhaps one person may be able to lead as well as write down the basics, and even list the proposed solutions during brainstorming by the parties. Some folks cannot do all this. You may need to find another special person who can take notes and work with the co-leaders to transfer faithfully into writing the basic points and ideas. That person is a "scribe."
- *Empathy* - A trained and perceptive leader can consider the views of the other side, including: "Put yourself in their shoes," and, in a twist: "Would you take the deal you offered them?"
- *Flexibility* - Leaders may need to teach the participants what is "conflict" and its inevitability and the basics of dispute resolution. In teaching, they learn vocabulary and more sophisticated concepts of "conflict resolution."
- *Open-mindedness* - Good leaders and participants listen to understand, not to argue. The leader can model good practices.

For example, once you understand a point, prove it by rephrasing — positively — the argument that you have heard. Participants and the leader can practice, model, and teach a willingness to listen to make each side's argument. This is important once you get to the stage of brainstorming solutions.

- *Cordiality* - A leader should understand the importance of avoiding personal attacks. Appearances matter. Acts of respect and courtesy encourage discussion, progress, and resolution.
- *Vigilance* - Leaders must be vigilant, understanding the process works only when they can maintain civility and order. Leaders must use their senses to detect underlying issues. The leaders and participants should remain alert to any changes (rhetorical, tonal, physical cues) that the effort is turning to incivility, personal attacks, or violence. In today's world, we must be alert to any cues or threats of violence.
- *Communication Skills* - While leaders must promote an environment of listening, a good leader also allows — and encourages, where proper — the participants to speak while enforcing the basic ground rules. The leader knows when to speak and when to encourage others to speak. For some people, a speech may amount to one or two words, spoken clearly as they make eye contact with the audience — if they are able — and otherwise state their position, as succinctly as

they wish. They will communicate in whatever method their abilities allow. Help your participants in practice to find the best way to make clear their position or answer.

- *Judgment* - A skilled leader knows when and how to permit sufficient venting but not let it get out of hand. Well-trained guides can recognize, manage, and even ignore side disputes by returning to goals with positive statements, continuing to move the dialogue and work forward to the solutions stage. And sometimes leaders need to take the blame so the stakeholders can stay calm and carry on.

When asked why his warring friends asked Carlos to solve their problem, Carlos reflected on his style of listening and helping:

"I like people. I'm genuinely interested in what they have to say. People trust me.

"I can tell jokes. You can tell a lot of jokes; but be sure you don't offend anyone with your jokes. You kid back and forth, and they get to know you and trust you.

"Use all your senses. I can read people.

"I get invited to just come and talk and relax people.

"I've been cutting hair for more than 50 years. I get to know the people. I know their religion and their education and their beliefs. I know the person.

"I'm just a high school grad, well with a bit of junior college. I like to tell people: I graduated from the University of Nasa Road One.

"It's about trust. Trust is really important. If people

think you are BS-ing them, you cannot succeed. Tell them what you feel. People sense when you are lying or not telling the whole truth. Trust is really important."

In the case of the repentant thief and the stolen gold watch, Carlos' father was in a superior position to resolve the matter. Augustin Villagomez was a trusted, community leader. His decision in the Case of the Repentant Thief had the impact of law in the view of all concerned. Carlos witnessed the entire episode and recalled one day, as he was relaxing in the second barber chair:

"You know, I was there, I was in my twenties, I'd just come home from Vietnam, in the Navy. I was still living in their garage, in the back. I was there when the man with the watch came. I remember the tone of my dad's voice when he decided what the guy would do, and my dad wasn't going to keep the watch. His tone of voice when he said: 'no lo quiero;' he said he did not want it. And when he said, 'Ya se puede ir,' just like that he said, 'now you can go.' And he did not hesitate, and he told that thief what he must do. We were all listening."

Carlos shook his head remembering more than 60 years past. "My Dad could've had his watch. And he didn't want it. I will always remember that.

"My Dad had this tone of voice; you knew he meant what he said. He had two brothers like him, things were yes or no. You do right. His voice, the way he was, he got respect for who he was.

"I remember when we'd walk to church, no side-walks where we lived, but there were paths to the church. And these 'pachucos,' you know, these wise guys, bullies, they'd always block peoples' way and make them go around and get off the path. They'd even hassle old people and the old ladies going to church, everybody. But when my Dad came by, he would look at them and say – in that voice of his, wise, fearless, and calm – 'Con permiso,' you know, the polite comment, 'with your permission,' but he didn't say it as a request. No, it was not a request. He just said it. It was a statement. And they always moved out of his way. Everyone knew. My Dad meant business."

Augustin Villagomez was true to his own code and beliefs, and elegantly resolved the case of the pilfered gold timepiece. The solution may not have suited others, but the particular penalty – that the thief must wear the stolen watch and tell people what he had done, relying on the thief to fulfill this penance – met the needs of Mr. Villagomez. Importantly, in the belief system which Mr. Villagomez closely shared with the thief, the solution met the everlasting needs of the thieving co-worker.

Mr. Villagomez did not place value on desires for the possession of the worldly good, wrongly taken from him and physically lost to him those many years. He understood the thief's needs (forgiveness and salvation) and wants (the easiest way out) every bit as well as he understood his own need for justice.

Neither man may have gotten his worldly wants. But one can certainly consider, from their vantage points and belief systems, that the resolution decreed by Carlos' father met their needs.

4

RESPECT THE PARTICIPANTS

Do you know any person in this world, or even beyond, who does not want to be able to safely express their opinions, to be respected, heard, and considered? Ground rules give everyone the right to be heard in ways that do not harm others. Each participant plays an important role in the process and outcome.

Properly enforced ground rules allow each participant to explain their position, however they choose to express themselves.

Alan Shepard and Edgar Mitchell, two very different men, were regular Carlos clients. They shared tight space on Apollo 14 to the moon, where they rigorously labored and brought back a huge cache of lunar material from intense and strenuous work on the moon's surface. Shepard took famous photos of Mitchell, including a memorable shot of Mitchell reading a map as he walked, and one of the world's most celebrated "selfies" which included Shepard's own shadow artfully extending in the foreground of Mitchell's iconic pose with the American flag. (It's the only photograph depicting Shepard's presence on the moon's surface.)

Astronauts Mitchell and Shepherd were Naval aviators. Shepard was world famous even before he went to the moon; he was the first American in space. He frequently engaged in his favorite sport of golf with celebrity friends, like Bob Hope. He was a dear friend to Carlos and was an Admiral by the time he was operating a popular Coors distributorship, benefitting from Carlos' significant experience in the world of beer gardens. Carlos and Admiral Shepard spent months traveling from bar to bar as the once reticent airman learned from Carlos the business and art of talking with bar owners and customers.

Mitchell was well-known in the NASA area for his dedicated help during the Apollo 13 Mission to educate the crew on the unique challenges and art of handling a Lunar Module (based on his simulator work) with a damaged Command Module still attached. Captain Mitchell was best known in the Barbershop for his constant ESP demonstrations, to admiring audiences.

He used his mind to demonstrate his paranormal powers in moving Carlos' combs and pencils. Several ladies present claimed the combs may have moved a bit. Carlos says they never did. Mitchell later scheduled a program with invited friends to observe additional paranormal activity. Carlos attended, and he says nothing happened. Mitchell dedicated a good part of his life to investigation of paranormal activities and locating signs of life on other planets.

We know from Barbershop talk that the space program and the highly regulated world of spaceflight used these astronauts and their strong personalities for multiple purposes, including a demonstration of the indomitable spirit behind human space exploration. Mediation provides participants that key sense of autonomy, a degree of control over the process and the outcome. Success can rest in the actions of mediation participants; they have an important role. The mediation participants accept responsibility with others for creation and maintenance of a safe environment of respect and listening, with basic, agreed ground rules.

As a starting point, in mediation, the mediator guides everyone to introduce themselves and agree to basic ground rules. Throughout the mediation process, leaders and participants are encouraged to reference and enforce the simple ground rules.

Mediation is not a competition. There's no declared winner or loser. Mediation participants determine their own fate in a process they build, with a focus on creatively considering solutions, then critically analyzing the ideas/proposals. The participants rightly feel they play key roles in the outcome outcomes, including their agreement to rules controlling the conduct in the process and the respect afforded to each participant. The rules empower each participant to share ideas, to decide how they will participate, and to take responsibility for the decision-making process.

Empowering people promotes acceptance of the outcome, consistent with the work of Edward Deci, a psychologist who found that intrinsic motivations, rather than external rewards, are superior and effective methods of motivation. Deci's research, supported by other work and studies, shows us that the best way to motivate people is to "support their sense of autonomy."[2]

When we join with other participants in the design and embrace of the process, with voluntary agreement to simple ground rules, each participant strengthens the parties' willingness to follow the ground rules and to later carry out their agreement.

At the outset, get agreement to the Ground Rules:

1. No putting down. Show respect.
2. Listen actively. No interruptions.
3. Make your best efforts to resolve the problem.
4. Carry out the agreement once you come to it.
5. Maintain confidentiality, consistent with all legal requirements.

If a representative of one of the parties refuses to agree to very basic ground rules, do not bother to try to impose the entire process on such a person. What can you expect from a person who will not agree to rules which require common decency and paying respect? You can expect them to intentionally subvert the entire process and repeatedly violate the rules, including "listen for a reasonable period of time" and "take turns speaking."

The ground rules put the participants in a position of control over their destiny. This autonomy gives the participants a great opportunity to enjoy a protected environment where their voices will be heard. They can express themselves. If you create and maintain the mediation process, providing an environment where the participants feel protected, respected, and fairly treated, you can make progress, and enhance the chance for a settlement that will be carried out. Why? Because the parties had a choice in the outcome.

When you clearly confirm agreement to the ground rules, you also secure everyone's agreement to respect the people as well as the process. Whether in a quiet conversation, in a practice session with imaginary issues, or in a multi-party, massive conflict resolution, participants can truly sense the protection afforded when someone else comes to their defense in enforcing their rights. You will see immediate results when decision-makers understand that everyone is part of the enforcement of the ground rules, in practice sessions every bit as much as during mediations. Quietly, everyone builds confidence, step-by-step, as they experience the protective benefits of the process and environment they have created, in a classroom, in a conference room, in a virtual space – or in space, as the world discovered during Apollo 14.

The Apollo 14 moon landing was fraught with challenges, any one of which might have caused a decision to abort. Personnel on Earth and in the spacecraft overcame a cascade of issues at key times. When Shepard safely landed his craft on the moon and later stepped onto the moon's surface, his words seemed to summarize the extraordinary team efforts, including the dramatic efforts required to solve the host of last-minute technical issues as well as Shepard's years-long determination to overcome his medical issues to stay with the U.S. Space Program, undergoing dramatic, experimental, successful surgery.

Shepard's first words on the moon identified himself as there, "And it's been a long way. But we're here." He and Mitchell worked to near exhaustion on the surface. Shepard famously took a moment to prepare and swing a cleverly fashioned golf club at golf balls, missing the first. He connected on the second ball. He had arranged with NASA for packing a small, special golfing "club" attachment as well as the balls he could carry to the surface. (Yes, Apollo spacesuits had pockets.)

Ed Mitchell, too, gave his own, unique stamp to his mission to the moon. After the mission, he revealed to the world that he had conducted experiments during the mission to try to telepathically communicate with friends.

5

LOOK TO THE HEART OF THE MATTER

A Barbershop story illustrates the importance and beauty of Mediation Step One: Identify the True Problem. Every person comes to mediation with an identified issue or problem they say they want to solve. The trick is to discover the real issue. Problem-solving in mediation can uncover deeper problems which require resolution. Mediation can reveal the heart of the controversy or problem.

Wise and caring people surround us with elegant

solutions to our problems; we just need to recognize them, stop, and listen.

Here is a great story from the chair of Jesse Salinas at the Barbershop. Jesse asks thoughtful questions and draws stories from the quietest of the astronauts. They genuinely listen to Jesse, too, when he talks about his work in Galveston as part of a group of friends who formed "The Galveston Golf Cart Society" for helping the community. The group members plan and perform charitable volunteer projects, cleaning up the beach, delivering goods, and engaging in quiet, heroic efforts to make lives better on Earth. With Jesse's kind style, modest astronauts can be encouraged to tell their stories.

Jesse encouraged a heroic war hero Shuttle Commander to tell the story about the time the Commander and his beautiful, resourceful wife teamed together to solve a problem while she was on the ground and he was on his last scheduled mission in space. The resolution of the first, simpler issue set into motion extraordinary events which revealed a greater issue which was superbly resolved at the White House, with the President of the United States acting as mediator. The result had remarkable impact.

More than once, I have had the honor of being in Carlos' shop as Master Barber Jesse cut the hair of Naval Academy graduate, combat pilot, test pilot, and astronaut Mike Coats. Navy Captain Coats flew 315 combat missions in southeast Asia. In addition to his service as a pilot's pilot and astronaut, he served as acting Chief of the Astronauts office. After service to Lockheed, Commander Coats was asked to return for what he describes as "the best job in the world": the Director of the Johnson Spacecraft Center.

At the beginning of his second space mission, serving as Commander, with all gear and a few personal items properly packed and stowed, the astronaut had consulted his reserved, beautiful wife Diane with the idea of designating "something" from the crew to be flown for the President. President George Herbert Walker Bush, the youngest naval aviator in World War II, was a huge fan of the space program. Diane Coats took a week to think things through. She and her husband were aware that the President had received numerous special flown items when he served as vice president. She strongly suggested that her husband find something small and beautiful among the carefully-packed personal gear (each member was allotted space for 20 small, personal items) as a crew gift to the First Lady, not the President. She pressed her husband to find a woman's gift. It seemed, to the thoughtful Diane Coats, a superb idea.

Why for the First Lady?

"Because if you tell the President you're bringing a surprise gift for Mrs. Bush back from space, we'll all be invited to the White House," was the wise wife's reasoning.

So Commander Coats surveyed the crew; one had a very handsome, small, gold Space Shuttle charm packed aboard his personal gear. The astronauts decided to all split the cost of the gold charm and agreed that it would be perfect for Barbara Bush. As Mrs. Coats presciently planned, it came to pass. In orbit, as hoped-for, President Bush called the crew.

Now the ordinarily private and quiet Diane Coats was quite vocal and determined that her dream would come to life. She had coached her husband and was now together with the other astronauts' wives, listening intently to the ground link of the presidential call to the crew in orbit.

"The wives are watching," Coats tells the story, as he recalls waiting and waiting to insert his casual remark. "And my wife is waiting, and thinking 'Oh no, it's too late, they're signing off, he's not going to…'"

Then, as the President was saying his goodbye, just as the Commander knew his wife must be urging him now, back on Earth, Coats replied in a goodbye that they were returning from space with a little gift packed for the First Lady.

"That's fantastic!" the President exclaimed. He insisted the crew come to deliver it in person.

"Come here with your wives as soon as this one's over."

After missions, the usual practice was quite clear: quarantine post mission. Not this time. After this mission, the crew and their wives were in D.C. within days of landing. They received a separate phone call to please come early so that Mrs. Bush could give a most memorable, personal White House tour.

In the Lincoln Bedroom, Mrs. Bush went to the window, and called out to ask her guests over. White House tourists stood below. She tapped on the window. The crowd went happily wild and the First Lady enthusiastically waved greetings back.

"I love to do that," Mrs. Bush said, beaming with happiness.

Following tea with the First Lady, and after presentation of the very well-received gold shuttle charm, the President hosted everyone in the Oval Office.

Quite the trip.

Diane Coats quietly left behind a second gift in the Bush White House. She had prepared a beautiful dog biscuit in the shape of a Space Shuttle, packed in a shoe box. The biscuit survived frequent openings and examination at multiple White House security checkpoints. The still-intact biscuit-in-a-shoebox was left in the dog's room, which the happy group visited along this memorable tour.

Very soon after what would certainly seem the trip of a lifetime, Commander Coats got another call from the White House. Would the crew and wives please return for a State Dinner?

Invitations accepted.

Diane Coats was a very beautiful woman. She did not own a ballgown, but they found an appropriate one in the City, albeit three sizes too large. In the very short time remaining, the gown was taken in and the crew and wives were whisked back to the White House.

The Cinderella story continues, as Commander Coats recalls his beautiful wife outshining the movie stars. You can picture war hero Commander Coats in full dress uniform and his extraordinary wife standing in the receiving line at a White House State Dinner, in between Audrey Hepburn and Bob Hope. Next in line is the Prime Minister of Israel who is standing next to the President.

Commander Coats is thinking "He won't recognize me," as the President's gaze wanders over the line. Oh, yes indeed, the President of the United States has remembered the thoughtfulness of Diane Coats.

Commander Coats recalls the President as he spots and calls out, "Mike and Diane!"

The President, quite tall, is calling out over heads, and then turns to explain to the Israeli Prime Minister the story of the astronauts' visit with particular, fond memories of the Shuttle Dog Biscuit. Mike Coats is convinced that the State Dinner Invitation would not have occurred but for the First Family's delight in Diane's gift for the First Dog.

As Commander Coats reminisces wonderfully about his late wife, we learn there is even more to this story about the love of his life (from the first time he saw her) and what her thoughtfulness brought about. Couples were split for the seated dinner. Audrey Hepburn, Dolores Hope, and Mike Coats sat at the President's table. The President wanted to talk about space travel. He leaned over Audrey Hepburn for more personal conversation with Commander Coats.

"When are you going up again, Mike?"

"I promised my wife, this was it. You see, after the Challenger… We lost a lot of friends on Challenger…"

The President – and former World War II naval flier – pressed on.

"Do you want to go?"

Coats said yes.

The President replied, "Let me see what I can do."

President Bush crosses the ballroom. Coats observes him seeking out Diane. She is listening, quite intently, to the President of the United States.

"She's frowning at me," the astronaut recalls. But then he says, there is more talk, and he thinks he sees her smiling across the ballroom. Bush returns to his table and leans over to Coats, with confident pleasure, noting, "I think it's a go."

"Mr. President, what did you tell my wife, what could you have said to convince her, she's…"

The President replies, "That's between her and me."

Throughout dinner, President Bush returns often to the topic of space travel; it was such a treat to have the crews visit, he says, lamenting "What a shame they all don't come here after each mission."

The President asks, "Why can't every crew get to come here?"

"Well, sir … you're the President," Commander Coats succinctly replies.

So, after the extraordinary meal, and still in the White House, Commander Coats takes aside his wife and asks her how it was possible for the President to persuade her to change her mind.

She replied only, "We are invited back afterwards."

Mrs. Coats' generosity in recognizing the importance of her husband's unfulfilled mission combined with her considerable powers of thoughtfulness, empathy, and strategic thinking, did more than bring to reality the dreams of a White House visit. Her ideas, strategies, and generosity produced a cascade of wonderful results, which required deep listening and thought by all of the participants to this mediation, including the President of the United States, the appropriate mediator in the middle of a State Dinner.

The original agreement between the Commander and his wife was based on his deference to her great desire that he'd never risk being lost on another mission. Varying that agreement required presidential understanding that

Mrs. Coats' desire to shelter her husband from possible harm could be overcome with a gesture from a respected figure who could remind her of Commander Coats' need and desire to complete his mission service. The story is one of a true and loving partnership.

For the rest of President Bush's term, every crewmember and spouse received a White House post-mission invitation. Diane Coats was the quiet force which instituted a broader tradition most astronauts – and the country – had missed. The Commander reminisced recently that Mrs. Bush wore the treasured, handsome gold Space Shuttle charm on a necklace in an official portrait, paired with her trademark pearls.

Mike Coats left the astronaut corps not long after commanding his third mission into space – and his third trip to the White House. He tells the story of playing horseshoes with the President in the Rose Garden. Following distinguished service to Lockheed, he was later asked to return to NASA and well-served the Spacecraft Center as Director. To this day, he still describes that job as "the best in the world."

Develop Your Listening Skills

In problem solving, listening trumps talking. Set a goal to listen more than you talk so you can ask an intelligent question. Even if you choose not to ask the question, the exercise helps you learn and create the appearance of what becomes the truth: you begin to listen. Many over-eager speakers learn to write the word *listen* or the acronym W.A.I.T. (Why Am I Talking?) in a place where they alone can see it.

Once you create the atmosphere of respect, you will be able to gain insight into the nature, facts, and history of the problems; the personalities, needs and interests of the participants; and the possible solutions. Your information-gathering will serve you well, by fostering good relationships and giving you credibility when you show your ability to understand the other parties' positions, even if you do not agree. Your respect in understanding the other participants will ordinarily be answered with respect for your position.

What is "Active Listening"?

We listen actively by putting our minds in the position of listening to understand, not merely to argue.

Listen as if the answer matters, with eyes focused, body language creating the impression of interest. Avoid crossed arms, interruption, yawning, or turning your back. Write down words that are often repeated and ideas that sum the concepts. Listen so that you could, in turn, make the speaker's argument even more clearly than the speaker.

Even if you do not wish to listen, create the appearance of doing so. Pretend. Artifice prompts true listening. You can learn, demonstrate, practice, and model the art of listening. Then teach others. By creating the

> appearance of listening, you are conveying respect.
>
> Active listening involves sincerity if you can, but requires maintaining the appearances of listening, even when you cannot be sincere. Active listening can be a draining experience and requires cooperation and time limits. Unquestionably, active listening requires practice.

The checklist found in Appendix B provides methods to aid in creating the appearance of listening. The methods convey respect. Remember, too, the independent, important advantage of truly listening is that the listener gains information and insight, discovering facts, positions and – if we study appearances and concentrate on the speaker and their team – motivations.

Please advocate and design a process which encourages all participants to convey respect by listening or by carefully appearing to listen. The appearance of listening does more than convey respect. It provides you the opportunity to use your instincts and gather information. Many times, little talking is best, particularly if little is known.

Develop Your Speaking Skills

While you will communicate much by active listening, you may very well want to speak aloud, as well, for many reasons. You may want to communicate – verbally – that you are listening. You can say, “I hear you.” Other people may prefer "I see what you are saying." Everyone listens and learns differently through their senses. Every human relies on preferred senses.

Get to know yourself by learning about the broad array of senses recognized far beyond the ancient list of five senses of sight, hearing, taste, touch, and smell. Modern science reinforces that paying attention and concentrating efforts can improve certain senses, understanding of emotions, and empathic ability.[3] Preparation and play-acting for mediation will hone your abilities and test the reliability of your newly developed skills and instincts.

Encourage yourself and your colleagues to approach each mediation participant with flexibility. Take the time to learn how to respect people's differences. Educate yourself on cultural difference, for example, in communication. Consider how you might best demonstrate respect, from the perspective of your audience, not from your own perspective. Learn to vary your communication styles. For example, your gestures or physical closeness to a person may be perceived as unwanted familiarity or a threat, although you intend only emphasis or display of trust and friendship.

You can respect people by adapting to their learning preferences. Some people prefer charts, graphs, lists, or photos to remember key points. Some folks rely heavily on colors; others cannot see the difference. Some avid listeners prefer to hear stories, well told. Visual learners might prefer a written checklist. Many people lack access to electronic communications. Have you taken their needs into account in your communication strategies?

Once you have had a chance to listen and learn

from a person, your instincts will tell you what styles they prefer. Encourage your listeners to talk. When it's time for you to speak, talk about what you know. Tell a story on yourself if you want the others to understand and know more about your motives and your organization's needs.

In being yourself and communicating, try to keep the following points in mind:

1. Simple, Short, and Story-Like - Shorter is better. Think before speaking. Take a breath. Relax and talk. And know this: smiling relaxes you.

2. Pointed, Practiced, and Prepared - Make your point. Wait for questions. Remember to smile. How to practice? Say phrases aloud. Repeat them often. Outlines are great. First impressions count. So, practice beginnings. And, perhaps, conclusions.

3. Calm, Casual, and Confident - Calmness is catching; people will respond. Use casual conversation. Confidence is relative; over-confidence is rude. Try for balance. Try being natural.

A Note on Logic

> Logic frequently fails in combatting disinformation. In an increasingly polarized, disinformation-filled world, you may find it impossible to effectively rely solely on logical appeals.
>
> How can we effectively inform others, counter disinformation, and persuade when logic is ignored? Find sources other than

> yourself or your circle of experts and leaders so you can make effective, persuasive appeals. Move outside your comfort zone and use the friends, loved ones, leaders, and respected sources in the minds of the folks on the other side of a disagreement. Do not limit yourself by using your old, familiar experts and information sources when the other side will not give credence to such sources.

Here is a pragmatic, bottom line on speaking: If you are asked to make a statement, use the time you have to prepare. It may be ten seconds. So be it: breathe, think of one thing (or three things if you're ambitious) which you want to say, pause, breathe again, smile.

If you have more than ten seconds to prepare: consider your story, your theme, your good intent. Then make the one or three points you wish to make. Once you practice the first phrase and the last phrase you have planned and you practice over and over, you will find that your middle phrase flows naturally.

In any discussion about problems and solutions, a trained listener can recognize negotiation strategies and tactics demonstrating posturing, gamesmanship, or some form of advocacy training. Everyone should use care in selection and use of strategies in the confines of mediation. The compressed space and time of mediation can magnify rhetorical techniques and gamesmanship. For example, "good cop/bad cop" is easier to identify. Do not outsmart yourself with fancy games or techniques.

You may be able to spot one technique, known as "*mirroring*," unless it's quite subtle. People observe other's habits, such as favorite words or gestures, and repeat them back at a later time, figuring that using a person's favored language or style will carry extra persuasive impact. Admittedly, mediation does offer a possibility for such tactics when people learn to carefully watch and listen to a person's words, phrases and body language. Do not abuse your observations. The tactic of mirroring someone else's conduct can sometimes be easily spotted. Such activity can also offend if someone feels they are being targeted or mocked for their identifiable habits.

What causes a listener to remember any particular point from a speech? Perhaps the speaker startles the listener with an unusual movement or statement. A lawyer lays down on the floor to ask a witness to reenact what they saw. Or a salesman plays a tune with lyrics that trigger a memory.

Anchoring is a technique for emphasizing one point. The shortened time span of a mediation adds opportunity for this very interesting method. You will observe *physical* anchoring when a teacher pulls a book off the shelf or moves to a different, identifiable spot and then makes a main point. Later, they will remind you of their physical move and what they said. A presenter can also make a main point with *verbal* anchoring, tying one issue or argument to another concept with a "cue" word. Consider what may be effective language for such verbal cues, such as "Every time you hear the word ____; picture the following ____."

Here is an example of verbal anchoring. When you hear the word "golf," picture astronaut Alan Shepard (whose favorite sport was golf) exploring the moon's surface on Apollo 14. You will likely associate the word "golf" in the future with a solid memory that Alan Shepard was an Apollo 14 moonwalker.

Trained advocates learn and practice many types of basic techniques to make ideas stand out. Listen for them. Understand these techniques are part of communication and persuasion. The following ancient, traditional devices work very well, whether used in a mediation, meeting between parties, or any setting. Consider these three concepts to add to your tool kit as you begin to enjoy speaking, as well as listening:

1. Primacy and Recency – People remember best the first and last thing they hear. Thus, make your important points accordingly. Most speakers, too, can memorize easily a few words for the beginning and end of their speeches. Practicing the beginning and end of your speech helps to create a great impression, coming and going. Remember to practice aloud; you will learn to hear yourself as others hear you; you will naturally change your speech from written format to a more natural, speaking format.

2. Ethos, Pathos, and Logos – Aristotle used three Greek words in teaching persuasion. Modern teachers of speech still refer to *Ethos*, tying your point to a recognized authority, relying on the source's ethical appeal of being liked, credible, qualified; *Pathos*, appealing to folks' emotions, whether they are sad, happy, moved by patriotism or love of a subject; and *Logos*, the appeal of logic. The speaker hopes to combine all three. Some teachers would add *Kairos*, referring to anchoring an argument to time and place. For example, a trained or instinctive speaker might want to explain the urgency or need for action "here and now," using current conditions as motivation.

3. The Rule of Three - In Western culture, many people are taught to think in threes. The concept dominates writing, tree planting, old-fashioned legal copies, religious concepts, and many varied occupations, practices, and teachings. Use the Rule of Three as your friend. Present three concepts at a time, when you can.

Develop Your Ability to Look Behind Stated Positions

In a mediation, once the introductions and obtaining agreement to ground rules are completed, the parties speak in turn to identify the problems or issues. A mediator might ask "what happened" and other open-ended questions, and everyone works towards creating the appearance of listening. Everyone will be encouraged to be open and receptive in trying to determine what are each side's issues and story. Everyone searches to determine what lies beneath a claim or story. What true needs and interests lie behind the stated positions? How determined are they, and why? What is affecting them? A listener tries to consider what each side considers as its definition of success. Do the parties have common interests and definitions of success? The parties and mediator all try to gain and gather information as they model "active listening."

They listen to understand and learn, think and then speak, in a constructive way.

For more lessons in public speaking see Appendix C, but they won't beat the lesson of why and how mediation participants Mike Coats, Diane Coats, and George

Herbert Walker Bush changed a prior agreement of no future space missions. To vary such a love-based agreement required presidential intervention and an extraordinarily kind, generous, and mutual recognition of each person's needs as well as wants.

In the barber shop, it's the best love story of all.

6

IN THE BEGINNING, BE CREATIVE

How do leaders solve problems? Neil Armstrong, John Glenn, and Carlos all understood Mediation Step Two: Solve the Problem with Creative and then Critical Thinking. When solving the problem, first be creative, then use your critical thinking skills to select the best solution to get the job done.

Neil Armstrong, the first man on the moon, kept his hair short, parted at his receding hairline when it was not cropped so close as to require no combing. The quiet, reserved gentleman told Carlos he wanted to travel, but his face was so famous he could not go out publicly and retain his privacy. He could not enjoy the great pleasure of anonymity in traveling and sightseeing. Carlos, as always, listened well. He then explained what a huge change your hair can make in appearance.

Armstrong said he wanted to travel in Mexico. Carlos recommended that the very-private man grow a mustache and let his hair grow quite long. Armstrong returned with long hair, but he could not grow a good mustache. Carlos bought a luxuriant, false mustache, trimmed the astronaut's hair and mustache into a Pancho Villa style, then dyed everything to near-black. Armstrong learned quickly how to properly glue and groom his new appearance.

The world-famous face was unrecognizable. He enjoyed a long and reportedly wonderful, private time in his travels through Mexico.

Carlos listens as well as he tells stories. He's all the more beloved for it. His reputation was such that one of the most famous men in history came to seek advice. Carlos listened to Neil Armstrong, indeed. But it was Armstrong who understood that he did not know everything; he had the wisdom, the presence of mind to know that good problem-solvers live and serve in every community.

Make Progress; Don't Slip Back

Consider problem-solving and resolving disputes as processes. Your work should constantly progress with transitions to new levels after a certain amount of important information is shared. Once the parties have identified and discussed the problems, disputes, or plans, the leaders guide the process to a new stage: solving the problem. Always be aware of the dangers of slipping back, later in the day, to the early stages of information exchange and identification of issues.

Brainstorm Solutions using Creative Thinking

In brainstorming, you must transition forward to a solution-oriented stage and not revisit old factual disputes or seek judgments to try to place blame. Brainstorming is a process to encourage openness and free flow of ideas while offering no criticism. In discussing solutions, a good leader encourages the free flow of ideas without ridicule or judging. This process requires either a writer you have chosen, or use of the leader or leaders, if you've found someone trained to be both a scribe and a leader.

The Importance of a Scribe

> Good scribes can list the possible solutions without judging them. Use your scribes to write down the ideas without making fun of extreme or impractical concepts. The wise scribe can

> quietly omit documentation of genuinely insulting or facetious concepts.
>
> A leader may also be a scribe, but you may need two different people. The leaders you select have a key job: maintaining a protected space of respect and dedication to the process, demonstrating calm perseverance in securing agreement to the Ground Rules in the beginning, and properly enforcing those Ground Rules.
>
> A good scribe can list outrageous ideas without appearing to judge or take sides. It is a difficult task, but an essential part of the process in listing ideas neutrally before entering the next phase of asking questions to test and select the best solutions.

Learn and model *creative thinking* to brainstorm ideas. After each side has expressed their view of the facts, the leaders then ask what can be done to improve the situation or to prevent a specific recurrence. The concept of no interruptions, no making fun, and the show of respect is key in this stage. Do not thwart creative thinking time with criticism. The leaders must be ever vigilant to avoid backsliding into the facts of the dispute. They must remind the parties that the process is advancing; you are in the solutions stage. Do not interrupt; allow free flow of ideas. Do not backslide into the facts of the dispute; remind the parties you are in the solutions stage.

Be Aware of Unconscious Tendencies

Studies demonstrate that we are more likely to consider changes that *add* features, rather than consider solutions that *remove* those features. People unconsciously reject "subtractive" solutions; we prefer "additive" solutions.[4]

How can we address unconscious neglect of ideas deserving, at least, recognition? Point it out. Make the participants aware of this human tendency. Focus attention on the fact that, while the proposal is indeed taking away something, it should not be lost in the list of ideas.

If a party seeks removal or subtraction by defunding or eliminating a program as a solution, encourage the participants to carefully direct their focus on the very specific proposal, recognizing it as subtractive. Then, ask the participants to use their imagination to see the world without the item to be subtracted.

While one party might be prompted to describe the disadvantages and unworkability of removing the institutionalized item, reflecting on the benefits to the known, established feature, another party could draw attention to the advantages of the removal in positive words, such as improving performance, earning respect, promoting savings, modernizing and advancing the involved organizations and persons into the future.

Test Solutions using Critical Thinking

Scientists use a variety of methods, inspirations, and senses to make theories, and then scientists test those theories or "hypotheses." They seek to determine whether their theory, when tested in appropriate and repeated experiments and practices in the reality of our world, holds true. If, in reality, the theory fails when appropriately tested, the theory is not valid.

Unlike certain well-tested, scientific hypotheses which endure over the millennia, untested theories dominate our human brains. Many people cannot change their opinions based on new information; their strong beliefs will not be shaken. And every one of us holds opinions based on untested claims, teachings of others, our impulses and beliefs, and our own, unscientific experiences.

What is "Critical Thinking"?

Critical Thinking is a process of thoughtful questioning – silently, in your mind and notes – of the information you are constantly receiving. You must take the time to learn and reflect, objectively, without passion or anger clouding your judgment, to face reality, and learn the facts and the other side's position, so you can make reasoned, rational decisions.

Critical thinking requires no abandonment of faith, but rather requires us to gain vital, factual knowledge, and understand the situation as clearly as possible, so we can proceed in a reasoned manner, consistent with our good faith.

When you criticize negatively, without thought, or speak via bad methods such as name-calling or personal attacks, you are *not* engaging in critical thinking.

Critical thinking asks questions to learn and gather more insight on such issues as the reliability of information sources, testing validity data, and learning what key information is missing. It allows us to recognize and prove that reliable facts can greatly differ from beliefs and opinions.

Learn and model *critical thinking* to test information reliability and solutions. Your mediation leaders will list, then ask you to test, your proposed solutions. (Good scribes discreetly edit the patently offensive ones.) Leaders ask the parties how each would work in practice, asking about advantages, disadvantages, and "How would that work – or not?"

The scribe and leaders will be refining the list of proposed solutions to reflect discarded ideas (which might have value in resurrection in whole or in part) as the process moves closer to selecting the solution or combinations of plans the parties can accept. The parties work with the scribe and leaders to further refine the list to those solutions passing the "workability" and other questions. Even if it works, will the advantages of the plan outweigh the disadvantages?

The leaders serve important functions in bringing closure and in recognizing when the parties have solved their problem. At times, parties steeped in an issue do not realize they have reached agreement or have difficulty accepting that a problem has been resolved with a workable solution awaiting implementation.

A key point during this joint effort on testing solutions: the parties are searching for a solution in a process over which they have control. The parties are struggling, working, and debating in order to determine what is best. No autocrat has declared what is a right or wrong solution. The parties, using the agreed, due process, will craft the solution.

Select the Best Solution

What's best? It's up to the persons involved. Be alert and realize that simple gestures can sometimes go far to solve complex problems; offers to apologize or agreeing to a previously rejected proposal or allowing parties to save face or provide tangible gestures of respect can be legitimate solutions. A simple solution may be the superior choice. Parties deserve congratulations if they agree to any resolution. Each party has their own idea of a win. The key is to find a result both parties feel is acceptable: is it better than the alternatives to resolving the problem? More frequently than you may suspect, parties settle conflict with genuine apologies, a simple press statement, or mutually giving up claims against each other.

Solutions range as far as our imaginations.

John Glenn wanted to fly into space, long past the age astronauts flew. He addressed the problem with a well-considered and handsomely executed solution, as described by younger Space Shuttle astronauts in Jesse's chair.

Glenn, an original Mercury 7 astronaut etched in history as the first American to circle the planet, was asked to speak to a fresh crop of Shuttle cadet astronauts. After an inspirational talk, he took questions. A newbie cadet astronaut asked: "Why did you never return to space after your historic mission?"

Glenn paused then proceeded with a smile. Standing next to the high-ranking NASA director, he leaned forward and started with an introduction sure to catch attention.

"I've actually never told this story."

He spoke from his heart. The gist of the story from the famous Mercury astronaut, summed by the fledgling, was that Glenn felt the real reason for his permanent grounding was his well-publicized insistence that the press be barred from his home, since that was the sincere desire of his shy wife. In protecting his wife, Glenn strongly believed he had so contravened the specific wishes of a very unhappy Lyndon Baines Johnson that the President ordered John Glenn grounded from further NASA missions.

As the decades passed, including distinguished service to his country as a U.S. Senator, Glenn still wished fervently he could fly again. The nearby NASA Director stepped forward and granted Glenn's sincerely expressed wish, with the condition that he must meet the qualifications.

He did.

Glenn trained hard, qualified, and traveled into space aboard the Space Shuttle at age 77 as the oldest astronaut at that time to so fly, 36 years after his launch into history as the first American to circle the planet.

Glenn expressed himself well and patiently waited for the right opportunity. As rumor also had it, and reported to Jesse, the decision was boosted by a direct order from then President of the United States Bill Clinton, who had received a similar request from the national hero and determined that "Senator Glenn is going to fly on the shuttle."

Persistence pays off.

Sometimes, it's hard to persevere, to listen with patience, to re-word someone's idea positively or to ignore comments which provide no assistance – and likely were never intended to assist the process. Don't give up. Consider the longer-term goal of keeping the process alive to achieve what the parties need.

Moreover, old-fashioned barriers are disappearing nowadays, aided by technology and flexibility.

A Note on Location

Virtual mediations in Zoom or similar virtual spaces are as successful as in person mediations. Adults may take longer than the elementary school children who resolve deeply upsetting, life-dominating disputes during the lunch hour. The adults might mediate in a physical location different from a quiet classroom or office during lunch hour, but adults, too, can learn to peacefully resolve problems at the barber shop or over a few beers at home, the night before starting a mission, or attending to details on the way home from the moon.

Virtual locations also have a distinct advantage regarding active listening. Taking advantage of your gallery view, you can observe everyone's actions and reactions. You may see unguarded moments. In online meetings, you can most easily listen and remind yourself to W.A.I.T. (ask "Why Am I Talking?") if you remember to mute your microphone at the outset. It is a gesture to help remind oneself to think before barging in or blurting out an unconsidered opinion. Others may notice you muted and view it as a gesture of respect.

Mediation carries endless possibilities. If you could see trained student mediators in action, you would experience faith that people trained to respect each other can work together to generate life-transforming solutions. The solutions can happen.

It happens for businesspeople in old age and for children on the playground, whose disputes can be more crippling towards development than anything many adults might imagine.

It happens in virtual spaces and in a variety of settings.

It happens for spacemen with personal dreams to fulfill, long after their famous missions are completed.

7

IN THE END, YOU MAY NEED TO LET IT BE

In life, mediation and problem solving, impasse and roadblocks always seem to crop up at inconvenient times. Carlos tells a story of an increasingly annoying problem at the Beer Garden that vexed his staff and customers alike. His simple resolution ended up benefitting barkeepers and beer distributorships nationwide.

Alan Shepard owned his Coors distributorship in partnership with a Korean War Navy aviator, who happened to be married to a member of the Coors family. Carlos knew from experience that the Coors cans tended to rust, and the Coors delivery folks were required to rotate the older cans at every bar they serviced, to promote sales of those cans before the rust appeared.

Carlos explained to Alan Shepard the disruptions and problems created by the Coors delivery drivers moving around individual beer cans behind the bar during business hours. The drivers took longer to perform the task than what a good barkeeper could do more efficiently, as needed. Carlos advised his distributor friend that the distributorship should stop the hugely time-wasteful process of rotation, which delayed the drivers' travel and delivery schedules. Trust the bar owners to do their job in handling the inventory, said Carlos. Those Coors delivery men, in rotating inventory, were disturbing the hardworking ladies and gentlemen behind the bar, and the hard drinking customers in front of it.

Maribelle's, a famous, waterfront, pink-roofed bar visible from the Kemah Bridge as it offered entertainment and games of chance, was also complaining. Maribelle herself asked Carlos to solve the problem. The disturbances and, in some cases, loss of privacy for customers, were hurting everyone's business.

Admiral Shepard asked Carlos to come into Coors' nearby headquarters to explain the problem. As requested, Carlos drove over to the local Coors distributorship to explain the business interruption losses. Who did he find waiting for him? None other than Adolph Coors himself. When Mr. Coors understood the disadvantages to his customers and the bars' abilities and desires to handle their own Coors' stock, he changed the policy nationwide, to the pleasure of all, including the drivers with one less time-consuming task. Turns out, the drivers trying to rotate cans had been disturbing bar patrons of all kinds, nationwide.

With their credibility firmly established with Adolph Coors, Maribelle and Carlos took on a new issue – safety. Maribelle asked Carlos to advocate for a solution to the problems her lady bartenders suffered while opening newly-designed Coors cans with a push-through, stamped opening, requiring a finger press, resulting in a hole with a ragged edge and sliced fingers by the servers who opened them. Carlos went to Shepard, identifying both the problem and a solution: use of a tab to distance fingers from the metal edge. Shepard was persuaded to bring the issue and proposed solution to the attention of Mr. Coors. Coors adopted the proposed change. The ladies at Maribelle's were especially delighted.

Carlos and his colleagues behind the bar long understood the importance of addressing issues and problems as soon as possible. Mediators, too, can be proactive in preventing trouble.

A major roadblock can be "Authority to Settle"

One roadblock to problem solving must be addressed at the outset: a barrier referenced in the Introduction. The issue is *authority*: does the representative have the power on behalf of his organization to solve the problem?

Apollo 14 moon-walking astronaut Edgar Mitchell was a world-famous, well-sponsored and serious proponent for his theories, research, and experiments regarding extrasensory perception, telekinesis, and unidentified flying objects. When such issues made headlines, including UFO origins, NASA chose to differ. It finally got to the point where NASA determined to make an official announcement to demonstrate that Edgar Mitchell did not have "authority" to speak for NASA, to eliminate possible confusion about the retired NASA astronaut's role. They added a denial to complicity in hiding evidence of alien life to boot, noting:

"NASA does not track UFOs. NASA is not involved in any sort of cover-up about alien life on this planet or anywhere in the universe. Dr. Mitchell is a great American, but we do not share his opinions on this issue."

NASA proactively distanced itself from any possible appearance that the famous astronaut spoke for NASA. We create a problem in any attempted dispute resolution if we mistakenly assume someone has authority to make statements on behalf of and agree to solutions on behalf of an organization when, in truth, a person with real authority is not present. Do not assume. If the people present do not have the power to discuss, negotiate, and settle the matter, you need to delay the start until the right people can become involved or give approval to the process.

Watch out for people blocking without a reason

Folks may also try to play games or wreak havoc with the simple rules and cause delay or frustration in hopes that no agreement will be reached on the basic ground rules. The solution: persevere and get agreement to ground rules. Do not go forward without the basic agreements; you cannot enforce rules to which the other side never agreed.

Roadblocks arise at every stage. Be patient and follow the process.

Ideas to break an impasse

If you have chosen an independent neutral to aid your process, recognize that a neutral can raise thorny issues and absorb blame, as a non-stake holder who refuses to take sides. A good neutral knows to reword earlier-stated concepts and reintroduce solid ideas. A trained leader can rephrase old ideas in a positive light and can discuss alternatives. An effective mediator can ask questions which call for testing of alternatives without judging or advocating. Here are a number of techniques mediators use to get past roadblocks.

Ignore or Forget

Consider, can you ignore the problem apparently causing the impasse? Perhaps you move beyond impasse by "forgetting" the problem; pay attention only to the positives. When everyone ignores a roadblock by detouring, the source of the problem may save face and understand the benefits of moving on.

Persevere

Keep trying. Just as parties should be encouraged to not give up too early, the leaders need support, too. Encourage them to not throw in the towel. Everyone should take pride as worthy participants to a process, a safe harbor they have created, with the great value of sustaining a calm, protected environment.

What if participants grow sullen, angry, or silent? Understand they are human and may be reflecting their frustration or anger in their reluctance to listen or speak or ask questions. Solutions can start with your use of open-ended questions always followed by engaging in active demonstrations of listening.

Ask a Question

If discussions have gone tense, silent, or stale, ask a question. At a minimum, you will gain information and insight. But, just as importantly, you will improve the relationship. The person who is questioned with respect and interest will feel rewarded, as demonstrated by multiple studies.[5] Individuals place great value on sharing information, including information about themselves. When you as questioner encourage "self-disclosure," the responder activates portions of their brain providing a sense of reward. As you reasonably and properly ask follow-up questions, the responder in the conversation perceives you as listening, responsive, caring, and understanding. You are aiding the responder in doing what comes naturally; we humans devote 30–40% of our speaking to informing others of our own subjective experiences.[6]

Take a Break from the Topic or the Process

Consider changing the topic for a bit or taking a break. Remember to maintain your good listening skills, and then use your speaking skills to apply the concepts of truly effective speaking to turn the topic from disagreement to topics on which you can agree.

Tell a Story

Storytelling can distract from stressful, problematic moments. Carlos saves his stories for the right audience. In his world, Alan Shepard remains a beloved figure, and Carlos seems to understand the cheering and distracting effect of these tales of a celebrity who gave special attention to normal, hard-working people who could connect the astronaut to the real world. Here's a favorite Carlos story.

Among the laborers in the NASA area, Alan Shepard exhibited special patience, posing for photos, making small talk, and joking. When Shepard returned from the moon, he wanted to just visit without being "on," and take breaks, when possible, to just relax.

Carlos hired day laborers for work on building and maintenance behind the Barbershop. They were working high up as Carlos and Shepard were walking outside. Shepard called out to the workers, joking around in Spanish. Eventually, Carlos let the workers know who was chatting with them.

They couldn't believe it; here they were talking to Alan Shepard! Every man overhead knew they were talking to the man who has just come back from walking on the moon. He was calling up to them, in Spanish, with the cadence and accent he'd learned from Carlos, to banter with them. The moonwalker fluently answered the workers' questions on what it was really like "up there," in Spanish, with perfect timing:

"Too Hot.

"Too Cold.

"No girls.

"No beer, either!"

Everyone roared from the sky above the astronaut on the ground, who had found respite in the neighborhood of the Barbershop and Beer Garden, much as Carlos provides us with friendly escape, stories and banter nowadays.

Don't Slide Back

Progress forward. Be on the lookout for backsliding. The leaders and all participants should be ever vigilant to move the process forward and avoid regression into old fights.

Address Obstruction Carefully

Avoid a direct attack, if possible, on the offender. Call out, in an impersonal fashion, the rehashing of old complaints and stories: "We are sliding back, it seems…" Do not reopen old disputes. Use simple, positive language: "We've discussed and identified the problems. Now it's time to move to a new stage: problem solving."

As progress is made, some folks will persist and try to re-argue old issues, reopen healed wounds. You can call a break and address them bluntly in private if the offender refuses to stop.

Manage Difficult Personalities

Even if you think you see strong egos around you, first take a good look inward. Have you given everyone enough time to listen and be heard? Consider: what's the goal here? Solving problems. The best atmosphere is one of respect and consideration towards other people and their interests. We look past their posturing and repeated claims to try to learn the answer to key questions: what interests are they trying to protect and defend? Look inward, too, to control your own sense of importance and your own behavior. We, as mediators, use and teach how to use the powerful tool of mediation by example. Unfortunately, we can sometimes demonstrate misuse of that power. Be a good example of restraint. We can always improve.

Everyone brings life experiences and skills to problem-solving. Learn to listen to voices of experience from diverse sources. Listening provides a painless way to curb egos. Selfless acts, such as protecting others from verbal attacks by calmly enforcing ground rules, will help the mediation and enable the parties to get what they need. Try to focus on problem-solving for mutual benefit. Remind the participants of the ground rule that promises everyone will show respect. Your acts of decency will calm most situations and help people experience what school children learn quickly: insults or personalizing the problem will not solve the problem.

Carlos has remarkable humility. By example, he teaches his friends to try to set aside their egos. Carlos explains his philosophy: "You know I am a barber. If you're in the service business… then, SERVE!"

What specifically do mediators do with apparent egoists attacking the mediation? A mediator will re-evaluate the roles of all participants. Who are the ultimate decision-makers with authority? Consult during a break, individually, with the persons with authority to settle. Ask if one of their own has a self-interest that prevents the party from making a reasoned decision with the true interests of the organization in mind. Asking the question may suffice.

A Note on Safety

> You can proceed with mediation with difficult persons; the situation is rather normal. However, you can proceed only so long as the difficult person poses no threat to the well-being of you or others. Civil mediation is not intended to cover behavior or credible threat involving law enforcement, mental health, or potentially criminal activity. Your attorney might serve as a guide, as well as an aid to your instincts. Of course, you must shut down any mediation where you feel, for any reason, it might be unsafe to continue.

Take a break. During your break, if everyone feels safe, pause to think before you call an impasse. Take a breath and focus on protecting the process. As you return to full session, find a good way to encourage the meekest to tell their uninterrupted-time story. Encourage everyone to focus on protecting others.

What's even more difficult than the person who demonstrates an inflated sense of self-worth? A subtle egoist will not flaunt their assurance of superiority; a careful observer, however, can sense it.

Here are some broad suggestions for dealing with challenging characters.

1. Reinforce and encourage everyone to listen first. Do not single out the potential problem-maker. Ask

everyone to: "Take extra time to listen now, so you can later help us sum what we've heard about these points."

2. Remind people of the option to take a break or just announce it as the situation may require. Emphasize what they may have forgotten, including the need to listen to understand, to allow time for reflection.

3. Acknowledge that mistakes happen. Take responsibility and give everyone respite before moving on. Apologize if need be.

4. Consider that you may be closer to a solution than everyone realizes. Find an area of consensus and emphasize it before taking the break. Use the break to consider whether some consensus exists; perhaps that consensus is more meaningful than everyone realizes.

Sometimes, we mediators can be the problem. The mediator operates under the same ground rules as all participants. Participants may need to check a mediator in their over-enthusiastic exercise of power. Resist the temptation to allow authoritarians to dictate your process or agreements. Mediation in the United States follows the traditions of the enabling documents creating the independence (The Declaration of Independence) and formation (The Constitution) of the United States of America, with goals of fairness, equality, and due process under our now-centuries-old establishment of "Rule of Law," instead of "Rule of Man."

So, don't slip into deferring to strong personalities just because they attempt to increase domination gradually, just as you should not ask your leaders to become authoritarian decision-makers. If you transfer ultimate decision-making to a neutral person or leadership team, instead of pushing towards an agreed decision made by the parties, you may promote chaos, unhappiness, and non-compliance from folks who were not part of the solutions stage. The parties should work together to choose the solution, with assistance from the leaders as agreed by the parties.

A Note on Lawyers

There are good reasons to use a lawyer for your important mediation activities, beyond how best to put important dispute resolutions in writing. The best practice is to discuss the possible settlement strategies before engaging in settlement talks, to understand what is legally possible, and how to best structure the resolution. You will want a competent lawyer – not the mediator – to capture the essence in writing; the mediator does not represent the parties and will not lawyer the agreement. In using mediation with non-profit organizations, consider also inviting diverse professionals, including lawyers, onto your charitable boards. Diverse boards benefit organizations. Good and generous teachers, lawyers, accountants, medical professionals, bus drivers, artists, barbers, cooks, and waitresses abound. Each person and profession brings something to the table. A good lawyer understands fair play and justice and understands the concepts in this book, including the key principle explained at the beginning, Due Process.

Do not try to lawyer any agreement. The parties should hire their own lawyers to record and capture any serious action in writing. Good lawyers can reduce the chances that the result will be plagued with disagreements over the agreement, and whether it is enforceable.

Listen to your instincts; if you sense abuse or danger, shut it down

Remind yourself to follow your instincts. If your gut tells you things are amiss or might get abusive of any person or the process, do not fear shutting things down. You can make clear that you are ready to continue with the substitution of a rational, rule-abiding representative with authority.

Lack of authority to settle is a reason to delay the work. If folks are merely toying with the process, violating the ground rules, and refusing to abide by them despite reminders, shut down the process. Such misconduct means a willful and intentional defiance of the interests of everyone involved or absolute incapacity to look after those interests.

Persist only when safely possible. You must make clear, to yourself and others, your determination to never tolerate violence, threat, or abuse of the process. In every stage: shut it all down if you have any doubt there might be danger associated with proceeding. Do not even start if you sense danger.

Carlos learned a lesson of eternal vigilance as he watched one day as a crew of local lawyers crowded into his waiting chairs grew increasingly vocal. He waited a tad too long to step in with a story. As he started to escort one hot-headed instigator out the back door, one of the famous trial lawyers was already a step ahead and pounced. Unlike movie fights, it didn't take long. Just a few punches, a bloody mess, and half the old men ran through the back door. The other half ran out the front. Carlos cleaned up the blood mingled with hair on the floor, after doctoring the customer's face.

8

BE CARLOS. BE GENEROUS.

Goodness is its own reward, but you may well find yourself rewarded for your kind acts in surprising ways.

When Alan Shepard appeared for the haircut confirmed from Apollo 14's return from the moon, as promised, in 1971, the shop was empty. The happy astronaut came straight from quarantine, still wearing a NASA flight suit. His hair was a mess. He walked straight up to Carlos, reached into his own pocket, and handed something to his old friend.

Shepard called to Carlos' mind the particular night they had shared some drinks under the stars before the astronauts entered pre-mission quarantine. Carlos and he had discussed what Alan was going to do "up there." In that pre-mission visit to the Shepard home, Carlos had asked of him "Do something, maybe write my name in the lunar dust." Shepard had grinned and said he would do something.

Until this moment, Carlos thought that Shepard had already carried out that promise by a very public request for a haircut on the moonwalker's trip back to

Earth. Now, the spaceman had given him something else.

Carlos felt a small, round object in his hand.

Shepard had autographed an orb and told him, "Take very good care of it." It seems Carlos' friend had taken to the moon more than the two golf balls left behind. He had more stored in a pocket of his space suit. One of them, autographed by Alan Shepard to Carlos, now rested happily with Carlos.

Carlos is a great example of how good people make our communities work. They spend their life in good works, charitable efforts, and helping strangers and friends, beyond their worlds of comfortable barber chairs, beer gardens, sage advice and listening. Carlos shares his wisdom and his bounty.

Carlos' philanthropy is legion and quietly accomplished. The COVID-19 crisis did not stop the giveaway and delivery of his wife's tamales. His family and his extended family of generous employees served thousands more in the hard winter of 2020-21. For more than 40 years, he served his Rotary community and their Sister Club in Mexico City. On a visit there, he learned of the great needs of a medical clinic built by a donor, who left it unfurnished.

Carlos proposed to outfit the empty clinic building. He came home and visited around with friends, including a popular local hospital executive, Raymond Khoury, who welcomed the request. The kind Methodist St. John's Administrator, who now teaches Hospital Administration at the University of Houston, had recently upgraded the hospital with brand new equipment, storing the slightly used, still state-of-the-art, monitors, beds, sterilizing equipment, wheelchairs, x-ray machines, and so much more. Mr. Khoury provided anything one would find at a modern hospital. The equipment and supplies filled ten huge storage units. Carlos asked at his Rotary meeting for an 18-wheeler and driver to drive the equipment to Mexico, all needed for the next Saturday. That mission was also accomplished with thanks to a generous hauling company. Carlos arranged for loading, with Rotarians and community friends pitching in with Carlos. They loaded the 18-wheeler to the gills that Saturday, packing every space with additional donations of supplies, including baby formula and diapers. The massive load departed, on time, with its vital contents secured.

An inspired ladies club held a fundraiser to help, too, honoring Carlos with a party in order to raise more funds, which led to more philanthropic work, as the community recognized the great need for specialized medical care for children with serious cleft palate and burn injuries. Fine doctors, specialists including dentists and facial surgeons, stepped forward to volunteer their much-needed services. Community members opened their homes to the families arriving with children requiring special attention and needing places to recover – sometimes for months before the children and parents could safely travel home. Decades later, these grown children write and visit Carlos as healthy, handsome adults, with children of their own.

Please, give back to your communities in the ways you can best serve. You can volunteer in schools and libraries to read or teach your skills to the next generations. This is your invitation.

What do you bring to mediation? All that makes you special: varied life experiences, humanity, and determination to learn how to use your capabilities and curiosity; mistakes and hard lessons learned; fears, impulses, desires, concerns; your desire to discover and understand more about our world.

With mediation experience and skills, you can teach concepts, practices and techniques enriching countless social, business, and family lives, and our communities at large. You will be teaching long-used, well-tested and long-accepted scientific, mediation and debate principles and methods, focused on problem solving techniques. We can benefit ourselves, the organizations with which we are aligned, and our children. You can empower children — and the adults closest to them — with the basics of critical thinking, brainstorming, active listening and speaking in a protected environment akin to mediation where all agree on simple ground rules.

As scientists continue to explore why people believe in untested theories,[7] mediators know from experience that education and training are keys to countering untested claims. We can and have effectively taught children how to use the modern scientific method to test hypotheses to see if a theory is true. Significant research demonstrates program successes in teaching schoolchildren the basics of critical thinking, to question and debate claims, to propose and test solutions to problems. Our schools use a wonderful variety of programs helping children to develop important conflict resolution skills.[8] Critical thinking skills are the antidote to unproven, untested theories which always arise in difficult times, with disinformation feeding on fear, anger, unhappiness, and distress. Without proper science and testing methodologies, children cannot distinguish unproven theory and disinformation from verifiable, factual truths.

Adults can benefit from the same training as children. Untested theories need not guide our existence. Mediation participants learn critical thinking, empathy, and other major life skills. Mediation practice quickly teaches the participants how to recognize negotiation strategies and techniques involving posturing, gamesmanship, or some form of advocacy techniques. Students of every age can learn, practice, and employ conflict resolution techniques to best serve their interests in a negotiation and brilliantly teach, by example, important skills and techniques to the next generation.

Experienced leaders can volunteer to teach a peer mediation course. Skilled speakers can provide lessons on the basics of public speaking to allow students to see and practice communication skills and learn to recognize speakers using manipulative techniques against them.

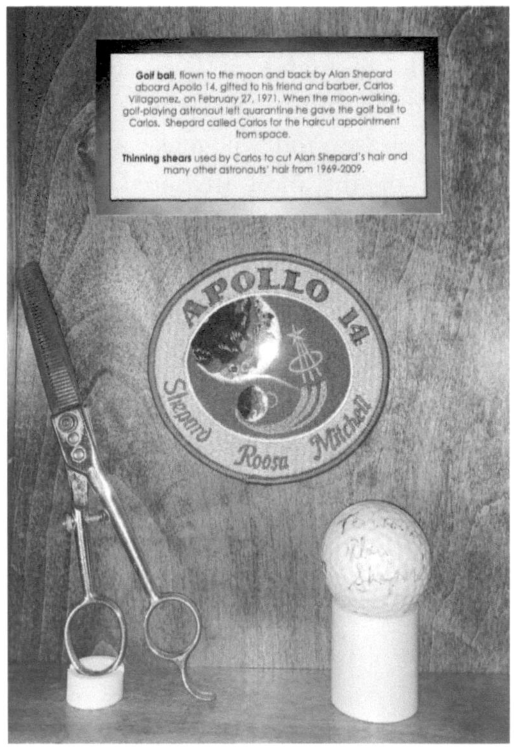

Be Carlos. His life of good deeds and problem solving has benefitted generations of deserving people. He tells the story of going in recently for needed surgery. In the hospital, a physician performed an examination and noticed Carlos' Navy tattoo. This led to the doctor's story of his grandmother's treasured account of survival in her youth. She ensured her descendants preserved her memories of a U.S. Navy ship with a "big gate" that rescued her as she was escaping what was to become known as North Vietnam, Indochina in the 1950s. She passed down the story of her life saved by the vessel as she ran aboard and the big gate closed. Her grandson wanted to thank every member of the U.S. Navy he encountered to know that he is alive and descended from one of the thousands of lives saved, due to the work of that storied ship and its crew.

Volunteer, please. You will make a difference and discover some of the most treasured and rewarding experiences in life.

AFTERWORD

Most people think that an extrovert who loves to talk has a genuine advantage in being a fundraiser. Research shows that when successful fundraisers meet with donors, especially major gift donors who give six- and seven-figure gifts and more, the donor does 75% of the talking, and a fundraiser does only 25%.

As a former practitioner who now trains both professional and volunteer fundraisers to overcome the fear of asking for gifts and be more productive, I emphasize that how you use that 25% of the time is precious. You must tactfully but firmly guide the conversation and obtain essential information that will enable you to align the needs, interests, and priorities of the donor with the mission of your cause.

It's not easy being a donor. Even those with great wealth must make difficult choices, not between the good and the bad, but between the good and the good.

There are more than 1.5 million registered non-profits in the U.S. — this includes all 501(c) designations from churches and cultural centers to food banks and disaster relief organizations. Though voluntary organizations endorsed by private contributions have existed in the U.S. since the mid-eighteenth century, they have only recently become an omnipresent part of American society. As recently as 1940, there were only 12,500 secular charitable tax-exempt organizations.

More than ever, the huge non-profit sector needs to come together to support each other's success in carrying out missions rather than competing for finite resources. Communication, coordination, and collaboration within the vast non-profit sector might sound simple, but it's definitely not.

Unfortunately, one of the great strengths fueling a non-profit's momentum — the enormous passion that each staff, board member, volunteer, and donor has for the cause — can and does get in the way of unfettered thinking and clear judgment.

Over the past two years, I've enjoyed leading more than 100 workshops, webinars, and board training sessions and have come to know hundreds of inspiring non-profit leaders. I always marvel at the genuine love they show for their organizations. This is expressed consistently and plays out in hearing, "But we're different, we're special, and no one else does what we do." Through our webinar series, we feature a variety of national experts on topics essential to resource development success such as major gift solicitations, estate planning, grant writing, communications, and others.

It's increasingly evident that we also need to strengthen the mindset and capacity of non-profits to be able to free themselves from built-in biases and become more adept at listening, understanding, and appreciating the roles of other organizations, and the vast potential to collaborate, achieve efficiencies of scale, and, ultimately, more effectively serve those whom their wonderful missions are designed to lift up. At the end of the day, we donate the precious gifts of time and money — which typically go hand-in-hand — to touch, improve and save more lives, not to perpetuate more organizations.

One of the advantages of my profession is nurturing relationships with colleagues all across the country who have become friends. I've been repeatedly asking them how we can empower non-profits to be more collaborative, and more specifically, who can guide us in this complex and sensitive area.

Enter Barbara Radnofsky.

She stands out for so many compelling reasons, I wondered why I didn't think of her much earlier. Her distinguished career has provided several decades of shining leadership in the art of mediation, conflict resolution, and simply bringing people closer together for mutual benefit. On two occasions, Barbara won her party's nomination for prestigious public offices representing Texas — U.S. Senator and Attorney General. She didn't win the general elections, but this even reinforces my admiration for her more deeply. When life goes your way, it's easy to do the right thing. It's the setbacks that don't build but rather reveal true character.

Barbara has continued to be a force of nature in promoting good causes, and non-profits have a special place in her heart. I've been fortunate to receive her mentoring and support as I launched my fundraising training/consulting business and wrote my first book, *10 Simple Fundraising Lessons.*

When I reached out to recruit her to speak as a

subject matter expert in our webinar series, she agreed immediately, and this sparked lively e-mail exchanges and phone conversations.

Recognizing the profound need to demystify the art and science of productive conversation, problem-solving, and forging paths for people and their organizations to move forward together, extending far beyond the non-profit sector, Barbara indicated she was ready to write another book.

We can't wait to apply this easy-to-understand guide to our work with non-profit partners. But the lessons can and should be embraced universally throughout a society which is losing sight of civility. It's a priceless resource to empower people in every field and discipline to come together to talk about the awesome challenge of doing more with less.

Jim Eskin, Founder, Eskin Fundraising Training

ACKNOWLEDGMENTS

This book was prompted by a kind request from one of the wisest teachers-of-leaders I know: Jim Eskin. This expert and pioneer in philanthropic and charitable gift-giving asked me to participate in a Webinar on this subject matter; his insightful queries, knowledge, and communication skills prompted me to put into writing these lessons learned, while providing wonderful opportunities to serve charitable entities, as Jim explains in his Afterword to this book. The book was possible and is offered with thanks to the criticisms and skills of editor Michaela Wood, talented review of Faye Walker and Leslie Eisenberg, encouragement of Lauren Radnofsky, Julia Radnofsky, and Robyn Williams, and to the wisdom and patience of my best friend and husband, Ed Supkis.

Dean Gary Bledsoe, Carroll Robinson, Nicholas Spencer, and Carvana Cloud – brilliant lawyers, leaders in the modern world of public service and non-profit efforts, working to create a just world – have been inspirational role models and supportive friends. Sherrie

Matula, an experienced and dedicated expert in education, political science and practice, including as public servant, provided much insight into theories, research, and the real world of modern education, particularly in the United States. I am indebted to Melville House and Melville House UK Co-founder and Publisher Dennis Johnson, whose wisdom and constructive criticisms improved my work. Any errors are mine alone.

In college debate, I learned critical thinking skills described in this book from colleagues in their teens and twenties. These friends, now acclaimed leaders in law, governance, statecraft, diplomacy, and charitable/educational fields, include Sylvester Turner, Philip Zelikow, and Linda Listrom, guided by University of Houston debate coaches Dr. William English and Bill Henderson.

In law school, Professor Philip Bobbitt taught world history, philosophy, international relations, and so much more in a 1976 law course entitled "Civil Procedure." Professor Bobbitt challenged us to learn, understand, and use the meaning and importance of "due process" to do our work: justice. He conveyed a deeper understanding of the interdependence of law and strategy. "Justice" was one of the first biblical words I knew as a child. "Justice" remained on the wall in front of the familiar sanctuary where I was married, teaching us to "do justice, love mercy and walk humbly with thy God."

From the beginning of my law practice in Houston, I received advice, encouragement, and opportunities for volunteerism from the late, great Frank G. Evans III, a former Chief Justice of the First Court of Appeals in Houston, known here as the "Father of Alternate Dispute Resolution." Justice Evans' promotion of ADR in both laws and practice in Texas and the United States also led to his important, worldwide work developing conflict resolution programs and materials, on which my work is based. He taught how we mediators can teach children to mediate, the most satisfying work of my 40-plus years of law practice. Children learn and serve their schools as mediators most admirably. They teach others, in assemblies, in class, via art projects advertising their services, and in private talks with their friends, that mediation is a superior resolution to the ordeals of suffering silently or self-help which otherwise end in the grief of fighting, disciplinary action, and escalating problems with potentially disastrous results.

I thank Carlos Villagomez and his colleague Jesse Salinas, working to carry on the traditions and legacy of Carlos, for wise advice and many kindnesses. For more than 50 years, Carlos cut four generations of my family's hair, and he and Jesse cut our family's hair to this day. No Barbershop customers could have better friends.

FREQUENTLY ASKED QUESTIONS

What is your general thinking on approaching problem-solving? How do you create an environment that emphasizes mutual respect, active listening, and a genuine commitment to understanding differing viewpoints?

Teach and learn as you work to develop the fair and positive process we all deserve and are due. The skills you can learn include active listening, public speaking, creative thinking, and critical thinking.

You can create – physically and in spirit – an environment of respect, a protected space. Help all folks involved to agree to Ground Rules which emphasize civility and listening. No insults, use gestures of respect, no interruptions, make your best efforts to resolve, carry out your agreement.

Prepare, prepare, prepare, using your best folks who are trained to lead. Train them to help everyone create and maintain a comfortable environment of respect and, particularly, listening.

These are acquired skills. Prepare and get training. You can train yourselves if folks are willing to take the time.

What are the basic steps of mediation?

Step One: you identify true problems by planning and following a process to create an atmosphere of respect, with much "active" listening (yes, that's a thing) and good communication skills (yes, you can learn). You create an environment of mutual respect as you listen to each person make their points in order to identify problems.

Step Two: you move forward to solving problems. How? You use creative thinking (brainstorming possible solutions) and then critical thinking (to test the workability and weigh advantages and disadvantages of the proposed solutions to the problem). In Step Two problem-solving, you can enjoy a non-critical environment of brainstorming, followed by a clear move into testing the solutions everyone has brainstormed earlier. In determining if and how a solution might work, you will learn to effectively use "creative thinking" for brainstorming and then shift to "critical thinking" for testing solutions.

Boil it down, please. What does mediation do for us?

The mediation process provides a protected structure to peacefully resolve our problems in an atmosphere of mutual respect. We live in an ever-changing world, dominated by information, much of which is untested and unreliable. The antidote for unproven claims (such as conspiracy theories and disinformation) is teaching ourselves and others how to develop and practice critical thinking and related skills in our daily lives.

Problem-solving, dispute resolution, and collaboration between competing groups require learnable, problem-solving skills. Use whatever time you have to prepare to ensure you have dedicated people with authority, willing to engage in "active listening" during an established, protected process.

Setting and enforcing ground rules for civility allows for exchange of ideas, innovation, brainstorming and selecting workable solutions. Role-playing – "Put yourself in their shoes" – is key. Good people embrace "due process;" every American can and should learn the concept that we are entitled to fair notice and a meaningful opportunity to be heard.

Many people think they have the answers and prefer to talk rather than listen to others. How do we change that mindset?

Prove it to them via demonstration. Simple exercises showing how difficult it is to listen while talking help demonstrate the effectiveness – for individual, group, financial and business advantages – of listening. Listening breeds success.

These are skills which can be learned. These skills do not come naturally to most people. Children are quick learners once they see the results.

What other skills should we work on?

Learn to take good notes or find someone who can help you do so. They can act as a "scribe." Do not rely on memory; you can better ensure due process with lists and note-taking. Lists and note-taking serve fundamental values. In all aspects of mediation, as in life, safely preserve an idea which might later prove important.

Even people possessing supposedly photographic memories take notes; memory can be improved by note taking and visualization of your notes. For children, note-taking is a particularly great exercise, providing a sense of importance, purpose, and self-control.

You are your best judge of how best to keep track of ideas and concepts; everyone learns in different ways. At different times in your life, you will learn differently. We sometimes rely on our own methods to best remember ideas and concepts and lists; however, to ensure you and your colleagues don't forget a great bit of information, insight, fact, or idea that needs testing, make it easy on yourselves. Practice different methods for list making and see what works best for all of you.

Do not use communication systems unavailable to your colleagues; if they lack access to information or technology, either find a way to make it available to all participants or find a fair work-around. Ensure that your colleagues can share in the process of information gathering with access to records.

How much time should we allocate to the process?

Once trained in mediation, children can solve major problems, life-changing issues and problems, during the lunch hour. Adults usually take a day, depending on personalities and logistics. Zoom mediations seem to go twice as fast. They carry advantages and disadvantages.

The key is the preparation on each side beforehand in identifying and listing their issues and understanding the importance of agreement to ground rules.

Can you draw distinctions between the problem-solving challenges faced by charitable organizations and the problem-solving challenges faced by individuals and businesses?

Factually, yes; conceptually, no.

If I had to boil the process of problem-solving solution down to one word: Listen. While the factual issues and challenges may be quite different (every organization has its own unique people and history, just like every human being is different), a problem-solving discussion inevitably faces many common challenges, and therefore can benefit from common solutions.

Universal needs abound. Regardless of age of participants or the nature of the community or organization to which they belong, humans need and deserve respect, fair treatment, and opportunity to improve their world. Learning how to communicate with active listening is a great start.

What are your recommendations about how organizations – such as charities — should consider collaboration, or engaging in "stronger together" conversations?

If you want to collaborate, you need facts first.

Look to your own organization and then to your competitors, colleagues, and existing collaborators. Analyze and identify the true needs and interests. Once you understand the basics, consider outreach to people and organizations with whom you have the worst, most problematic relationships. Hard times make for friends when there are mutual benefits. Find commonality in a variety of ways, including problems, interests, and needs.

Understand you must always be gathering information and insight. Curiosity is a wonderful trait. Develop it. Brainstorm innovative solutions to meet common needs and interests. Perhaps the answers are not the same as what you originally thought you wanted or needed.

Recognize that are no winners or losers in mediation; some folks refer to the goal as a "win-win." Consider the varied benefits of the process as a "win" if your group can experience them.

The key focus is maintaining an atmosphere of respect and listening, as the listeners gain information and understanding to solve problems. Mediation listeners need to know they will have fair opportunities to speak. Trained speakers learn to use their time strategically; for example, to prove that they listen and understand other points, to develop a rapport, and to clearly convey their positions.

Emphasize everyone's need for an atmosphere of respect. Start by considering and listing all your stakeholders — everyone with needs and interests you serve. You will gain internal buy-in by frankly discussing your and your organization's needs. While desire for respect is universal, methods and styles of conversations, discussions, monologues, and dialogues certainly vary. Reject any practice which conveys a lack of respect. This will cost you nothing and can generate great reward.

What do I do if I am in a legal proceeding or need legal advice?

As you use this book, please know it contains no legal advice. Consult and involve your lawyer for legal implications and laws, including confidentiality and use of mediators in dispute resolution, as well as the process and effects on your organization.

For example, the issues of who has true "authority" to make an agreement and what conditions might be placed on the agreement, and what lawyers will draft the agreement, should all be ironed out beforehand. These are issues common to nearly every mediation.

If you have any concerns about fairness of the process, or if your underlying issues are legal disputes or might involve laws or the courts, seek a lawyer's assistance. If you have a dispute to resolve, your best practices can start and benefit by discussing the matter with counsel.

APPENDIX A - PLAY-ACTING SCENARIO

Engage in a Two-Act Play-Acting Scenario as an Exercise for each problem you identify. In planning a dispute scenario for play-acting a fictional problem, select something seemingly simple but with more serious impact than might appear to a supposed wrongdoer, who may have acted wittingly or unwittingly. We will never know the actor's intent; the mediation process does not try to read minds or judge guilt or innocence, but rather solves problems without judging or taking sides.

For example, one person may breach a trust, gossip about another, or have taken a small object from a friend's desk. The unhappy "victim" presumes a bad intent, while the supposed wrongdoer provides excuses either for the act or the unknown impact, or both.

Create a fictional dispute by preparing answers to these questions, and practice as follows.

- **What is the "true" problem (versus what it appears to be to most casual listeners)?**

- **What is the APPARENT PROBLEM?**
- **What are the HIDDEN MOTIVES and ISSUES?**
- **Who is involved?**
- **Possible Solutions: BRAINSTORM and LIST**
- **Test the Solutions: HOW WOULD THAT WORK?**
- **Select best win-win solution.**

Try two different methods (ACT ONE and ACT TWO) in your action once you have listed problems. The leaders are trying to find out, by listening for motives, miscommunications, differences, and common ground possible, the problems and hints of solutions which might allow parties to save face, receive an apology, think outside the box, or address a hidden issue no one realized until it was revealed, all disparate issues underlying the stated problems.

ACT ONE

The two disputants face each other and argue with each other. Each one has a secret bit of information they will blurt out that would REALLY help the other side understand: what is the true problem? Only the leader knows the bits of information. Can the audience or participants hear and discover the true elements at issue?

List the secret bits of information for each side that they plan to blurt out to the other side, which the audience does not know:

Party 1:

Party 2:

Time the argument at 30 seconds. The disputants will just talk on top of each other for 30 seconds, making and repeating their favorite, angry arguments, while slipping in their secret information.

Did the audience hear the bits of secret information that each side gave out? Did either side hear the important information hidden in all the argumentative talk? Discuss why there were difficulties and how individuals may have been able to overcome those problems.

ACT TWO

Start fresh, using **ground rules.** The leaders introduce everyone and themselves and then ask each person to offer questions they may have about the basic ground rules. The leaders then secure a strong commitment from each person to agree to the ground rules, after discussion of the purpose and meaning of the ground rules. If there is no such agreement, the leaders will postpone the opening until they can find representatives who will agree to the basic courtesies.

Do not proceed unless you have some agreement to basic courtesies or the process will likely fail.

1. No putting down. Show respect.
2. Listen actively. No interruptions.
3. Make your best efforts to resolve the problem.
4. Carry out the agreement once you come to it.
5. Maintain confidentiality, consistent with all legal requirements.

Hear from each side: What happened? What are the circumstances bringing us together?

After securing Agreement to Ground Rules, the leaders ask each side their version of what happened. The leaders will not judge or take sides. The leaders will likely need to remind the participants they agreed to ground rules by which they must abide. The leaders employ the principles of fair treatment and listening and offer neither judgment nor solutions. They may ask that each party summarize the other side's position.

Once the parties have a chance to talk and listen to each other, the leaders progress to the next stage: Brainstorming. Leaders must not allow the process to slide back into re-hashing of the dispute, which will not be judged by anyone. Rather, push on to brainstorming solutions.

Brainstorming Solutions

After each party has expressed their view of the facts, the leaders then ask what can be done to improve the situation or prevent a specific recurrence. Don't interrupt; allow free flow of ideas.

Don't backslide into the facts of the dispute; remind the parties you are in the solutions stage.

List, then Test, the Proposed Solutions

The leaders list the parties' various, proposed solutions they've summarized and ask the parties how each would work in practice, asking about advantages, disadvantages, and "How would that work?"

Select the solution or combinations the Parties can Accept

There is no right or wrong solution.

Interview the audience. Was anyone able to discover the underlying secrets that each party blurted out?

APPENDIX B - CHECKLIST FOR ACTIVE LISTENING

Physical cues: examples

- Body movement, such as nodding, smiling, leaning forward, and "open" body positions.
- Eye contact. Pleasant and appropriate — not a rude stare down just as it should not be complete avoidance.
- Equal treatment of all persons. Do not treat speakers differently.

Verbal cues: examples

- Expressions of encouragement ("uh huh;" "yes").
- Repetition and rewording to demonstrate understanding in a positive way, recognizing importance of word choices.
- Absence of interruption, a cue to encourage the speaker to continue. Silence is an action.

Neutral clarifying questions to demonstrate a desire to understand.

Use caution in such matters; many cultural, personal, and unknown factors may affect the perception of questions intended as neutral or clarifying to be, instead, a challenge.

- "Is this the same as or different from …"
- "How would you recommend we explain …"
- Other observations:

Brainstorm other neutral questions and comments and write them down to discuss:

Consider yourself, and write down what techniques work best for you to stop interrupting and listen:

Reminder: creating an environment of respect and the clear appearance of listening does more than convey respect; listening with use of repetition of points you wish clarified gives you a good chance to gather key information and is a great way to provide proof to others that you are hearing what the speaker is trying to say.

APPENDIX C - PUBLIC SPEAKING EXERCISES

Exercise 1

Look for "turnaround" issues. Listen carefully to the points – especially the negatives and criticisms of ideas. Listen and think.

Is there anything there which might be a blessing in disguise?

Is the supposed harm inevitable, requiring planning here and now to address, regardless of the proposed solution?

Is the supposed harm minor compared to the beneficial attention that the proposed solution will bring?

The answers to these questions may be "turnarounds" which carry the potential for using their logical underpinnings and bases to support the needs of all parties and groups involved. Look for that silver lining; expose and explain how these identified problems can be turned to great advantage if the parties anticipate, plan, and collaborate to address the issues in force, together.

Exercise 2

Consider your first few words as essential attention getters. This will cause you to pause, breathe, and relax before you start, because you know you want the audience to consider those first few words. The use of adverbs or verbs, with strong action in the first introductory words, is an effective device – if it's honest and true to your beliefs. For example, the word "when" is an effective, attention-getting rhetorical device when followed by dramatic action.

Exercise 3

Be yourself. Do not feel compelled to follow any guides, except rules of common decency, mutual respect, and civility.

APPENDIX D - MEDIATOR "CHEAT SHEET"

INTRODUCTION

Hello. This is _________ and my name is ___________. We are your co-mediators. During this mediation, you will both be given a chance to talk. We aren't here to judge you or take sides. When we finish, you'll come up with an agreement.

GROUND RULES

You'll both need to agree to some rules before we begin the mediation.

1. No putting down. Show respect.
2. Listen actively. No interruptions.
3. Make your best efforts to resolve the problem.
4. Carry out the agreement once you come to it.
5. Maintain confidentiality, consistent with all legal requirements.

Do you promise to agree to these Ground Rules?

LISTENING/REPEAT or REPHRASE POSITIVELY

To Party #1: What happened and how do you feel about it? Repeat or Rephrase.

To Party #2: What happened and how do you feel about it? Repeat or Rephrase.

SHARING FEELINGS WITH EMPATHY

To Party #1: Please tell me how _____ said they felt? Rephrase. How did they feel?

To Party #2: Please tell me how _____ said they felt? Rephrase. How did they feel?

TAKE A BREAK IF NEEDED

BRAINSTORM SOLUTIONS

To Party #1: What could you do to make this situation better? Or to keep it from happening again?

To Party #2: What could you do to make this situation better? Or to keep it from happening again?

TEST SOLUTIONS

To Party #1: How would that work? Any problems?

To Party #2: How would that work? Any problems?

CHOOSE A SOLUTION AND REACH AGREEMENT

- Sum the proposed solutions and get

agreement from both sides on the one(s) they've chosen.

- Write the agreed solution(s) on the school agreement form.
- Have the disputants sign the agreement.
- Congratulate the disputants.

REMEMBER: LISTEN! LISTEN! LISTEN!

ENDNOTES

1. For details, explanations, and a strategic look at these multiple, related concepts, read *Gain the Edge!*, MacMillan Publishers (2005), by Martin E. Latz.

2. For more detail, explanations, and scientific studies, see, for example, the research and writings of Professor Edward L. Deci and Pulitzer Prize winner Richard Flaste, former Science and Health Editor of *The New York Times*, summarized in *Why We Do What We Do*, G.P. Putnam's Sons (1995).

3. Consider researching further and learning more about yourself by reading *Super Senses: The Science of Your 32 Senses and How to Use Them*, John Murray Press (2021), by Emma Young.

4. Meyvis, Tom & Yoon, Heeyoung, "Adding to Our Problems," *Nature*, vol. 592 (April 8, 2021). https://www.nature.com/articles/d41586-021-00592-0.

5. Huang, Karen, et. al., Harvard University. "It Doesn't Hurt to Ask: Question-Asking Increases Liking," 113 *Journal of Personality and Social Psychology*, 430-52 (2017).

6. Tamir, Diana and Jason Mitchell, "Disclosing information about the self is intrinsically rewarding," *Proceedings of the National Academy of Sciences*, May 22, 2012 109 (21) 8038-8043; https://doi.org/10.1073/pnas.1202129109.

7. For a survey of this still-emerging field of study, see Karen M. Douglas, Robbie M. Sutton, and Aleksandra Cichocka, "The Psychology of Conspiracy Theories," School of Psychology, University of Kent, *Current Directions in Psychological Science* 2017, Vol. 26(6) 538–542.

8. University of Michigan researchers advanced the science of education by publishing key findings in June 2021, emphasizing the importance of teaching critical thinking associated with high school policy debate. "Competitive debate programs exist across the globe, and participation in debate has been linked to improved critical thinking skills and academic performance."

The new research, using Houston Independent School District data from tens of thousands of students, advances scientific understanding of the value of teaching critical thinking, listening, and speaking. The published research and findings show such programs provide help to students, boost grades, increase SAT scores in math and reading, and improve college readiness.

* Debaters earned higher GPAs (0.66) than comparable non-debate students;

* Debaters gained 52 points on their SAT Math exam scores over comparable non-debate students;

* Debaters gained 57 points on the SAT Evidence-based Reading and Writing exam scores over comparable non-debate students; and

* Debaters were 18% more likely to meet the College Board's benchmarks for college readiness than comparable non-debate students.

"Debate participation and academic achievement among high school students in the Houston Independent School District: 2012 - 2015" Tomohiro M. Ko and Briana Mezuk, Edu.Res.Rev https://assets.urbandebate.org/wp-content/uploads/20210607122625/Ko-Mezuk-2021.pdf.

ABOUT THE AUTHOR

Barbara Ann Radnofsky has taught and practiced mediation since the 1990s. A lawyer since 1979, Barbara is a grandmother, mother, wife, author, teacher, mediator, and attorney, and was named the Outstanding Young Lawyer of Texas in 1988. She retired from Vinson & Elkins, LLP, in 2006. Practicing on both sides of the docket, she's been listed every year since 1992 in Best Lawyers in America© in many areas, including dispute resolution.

Barbara co-founded the Houston chapter of the National Association of Urban Debate Leagues and has served on numerous charitable boards and as a peer mediation teacher in public and private schools. She and her husband, with many community members, co-own Brazos Bookstore.

www.ingramcontent.com/pod-product-compliance
Ingram Content Group UK Ltd.
Pitfield, Milton Keynes, MK11 3LW, UK
UKHW041956190726
13854UKWH00005B/2011

9 798498 272450